HENDON AERODROME
– A HISTORY –

HENDON AERODROME
— A HISTORY —

David Oliver

Airlife

Copyright © 1994 by David Oliver

First published in the UK in 1994
by Airlife Publishing Ltd

British Library Cataloguing in Publication Data
  A catalogue record for this book
  is available from the British Library

ISBN 1 85310 216 4

Printed by Livesey Limited, Shrewsbury

Airlife Publishing Ltd.

101 Longden Road, Shrewsbury SY3 9EB, England

CONTENTS

ACKNOWLEDGEMENTS

I would like to thank the many individuals, companies and members of the Services who have given their generous assistance during the preparation of this book by offering personal recollections, information and photographs.

Particular mention must be made of Wing Commander W.G. 'Bill' Simpson OBE RAF (Retd), RAF Hendon's last Commanding Officer who was the moving force behind the project and without whose help and encouragement it would not have been completed, and to Keith Ansell, CPRO Support Command, who put the whole idea into my mind; to Peter Flint who did a great deal of the preliminary research and unselfishly made it available to me; and to David Clucas who lent me his father's albums of 600 Squadron AuxAF at Hendon in the 1930s, and a lot of other valuable archive material.

Also thanks to the following: Clifton Adams; John Ackers; Dave Allport; Stanley Bacon; the late Lord Balfour of Inchrye; Ken Border; Rod Brewell; Earle J. Briggs; C.C. Burke; Dennis J. Carr; Tony Chapman; J.R. Clark; R.W. Cole; G.H. Coombs; Michael Crane; Arthur Dance; Albert Dean; John de Ledesma; C.V. Donald; Arthur Driscoll; Ken Ellis; G.E. Fletcher; A.R. Gilding; E. Glennie-Carr; F. Hugh 'John' Goodacre; Walter E. Gray; Peter Green; Roland Hammersley; Ted Hammond; M.P. Hanley; Peter Heaver; the late Sir Archibald Hope; Norman Jones; T.R. Jones; H.J. Kennard; Gordon Lipman; D.C. MacDonald; Frank R. McKee; R.E. McKee; Terence P. O'Halloran; Arthur Pearcy; Paddy Porter; François Prins; Douglas M. Reid; J.C.P. Thomas; E.S. Toop; P.B. Townsend; Anthony D. Ure: BAe; BBC; FAA Museum; *Hendon Times*; Museum of Army Flying; Post Office; Queen's Flight; RAF Museum Hendon; US Navy; 24 Squadron Historian; 23 Squadron Historian.

David Oliver
Arkley
March 1994

PROLOGUE

The first aviators to make use of fields at Hendon, situated in the countryside between the villages of Colindale and Mill Hill in Middlesex, some eight miles north-west of Charing Cross, were Britain's premier balloonists, Henry Coxwell and James Glaisher, who made an unscheduled landing on 25 August 1862. Coxwell and Glaisher had ascended from Crystal Palace some hours earlier with five passengers aboard their 93,000 cubic ft-capacity balloon *The Mammoth*. At dusk they took off from Hendon coming down at Biggleswade six-and-a-half hours later having reached a height of nearly 16,000ft. This flight was one of a series of eight ascents made for the British Association for the Advancement of Science. Two weeks later, Coxwell and Glaisher, flying from Wolverhampton, reached a height of over 30,000ft to create a record that was to stand for nearly forty years. However, it was some forty-six years before another aircraft, this time a heavier-than-air machine, was to be seen in the area.

In 1908, H.P. Martin and G.H. Handasyde began building a monoplane in the unused ballroom of the Old Welsh Harp public house at Hendon, a little more than a mile from where the balloon landed nearly half a century earlier, and close to the Welsh Harp reservoir. Unfortunately, during early trials in a neighbouring field, the 12 hp Beeston-Humber car engine, which was fitted with a large four-blade metal propeller, tore itself out of the aircraft; although there is no record of it being rebuilt, its constructors continued their partnership and three years later formed the successful Martinsyde Aeroplane Company.

Almost within sight of the Welsh Harp, another attempt to build Britain's first successful aircraft was taking shape in a shed erected by E.J. Everett, a director of a local firm of instrument makers, Messrs Everett, Edgecumbe & Co. This was a single-seat tractor monoplane powered by a 35hp JAP engine and assembled in the shed on the very edge of what was soon to become known as the Hendon Aviation ground. Various local companies helped with its construction, including Hawkers the Drapers of West Hendon whose seamstresses stitched the wing fabric. But although the aircraft made extensive taxi trials up and down the Hendon pastures over a two-year period, occasionally bouncing into the air, it never flew more than a few yards. Indeed it was soon christened the 'Grass Hopper' or 'Hedge Hopper' by the local enthusiasts who flocked to see its progress.

By 1910, Mr Everett had leased his shed to more successful aviators. However, the project was not a complete failure as one of the young volunteers who had assisted with the construction of the machine was C.R. Fairey, who, like Mr Martin and Mr Handasyde before him, was later to form his own company, the Fairey Aviation Company.

While these pioneers were taking their first hesitant steps in the relatively unknown world of aviation at Hendon, a successful young English car salesman, Claude Grahame-White, was attending Europe's first great aeronautical meeting at Rheims. Here he met many of the aviation giants of the day and made the fateful decision to learn to fly.

1 THE HENDON HABIT

GRAHAME-WHITE'S LONDON AERODROME

Seventeen years to the day after Coxwell and Glaisher made their unscheduled balloon landing in the fields of rural Colindale, Claude Grahame-White was born at Bursledon Towers on the River Hamble. The third child of a well-to-do businessman and grandson of a High Sheriff of Hampshire and one-time Mayor of Southampton, Claude grew up as a keen sportsman with a growing interest in things mechanical.

At sixteen, and in spite of his father's objections, he chose to become an apprentice to a Bedford engineering company and in his spare time was soon running his first business venture, a bicycle factory. Two years later, an uncle, Mr Francis Willey, a Yorkshire wool magnate, persuaded Claude to join his considerable business in Bradford, the Shipley Wool Combing Company. But despite working his way through all departments and being offered an attractive salary to stay with the company, he decided to start in business for himself by establishing the Yorkshire Motor Vehicle Company, which hired out a fleet of charabancs for pleasure trips.

In 1900, having sold that business for a small profit, Grahame-White accepted an offer to manage a friend's 20,000-acre estate in Sussex, turning a substantial loss into a substantial profit over three years before leaving to 'explore' South Africa with a £1,000 bonus from a grateful friend.

A year later he returned to England and his first love which at the time was motor-cars, establishing a West End motor-car dealership at Albemarle Street. As his automobile business flourished, Grahame-White turned his attention to aviation. He became a founder member of the recently formed Aero Club of the United Kingdom which was established to promote ballooning as a fashionable sport. In company with the Hon C.S. Rolls, T.O.M. Sopwith and J.T.C. Moore-Brabazon, Grahame-White purchased a 40,000 cubic ft balloon. However after making several ascents from the Battersea Gasworks grounds, he became increasingly frustrated by having to leave both the course of his flights and the location of landing grounds in the lap of the gods and so he began taking an increasing interest in heavier-than-air flying machines; these were then in their infancy following the Wright brothers' historic first flight of 1903.

In August 1909 he attended Europe's first great aeronautical meeting at Rheims where he met

France's aviation heroes including Henry Farman, an English-born naturalised Frenchman, the American Glenn H. Curtiss and Louis Blériot, the latter fresh from his historic flight across the Channel made only a month before. It was here that Grahame-White purchased his first aeroplane, a Blériot XII, which he himself helped to assemble at Blériot's Paris factory. Eight weeks later, he made an unauthorised, albeit short, solo flight in his Blériot (christened *White Eagle*) from a military parade ground at Issy-les-Moulineaux. He then took a course of flying lessons at the Blériot School of Flying at Pau in southwest France becoming the first internationally-recognised British Pilot with the award of Aéro-Club de France Certificate No 30 on 4 January 1910. He immediately ordered six Blériot Type XIs and established his own 'British Aviation School' at Pau. Grahame-White then returned to England, displaying something of the showman that would make him famous, by towing his Blériot XI behind a car through the streets of London, before making his maiden flight in his own country from Brooklands on 13 January. The main reason for his return was to find a suitable site for his proposed British flying school, preferably within easy reach of London. A week later his Blériot was being re-assembled in the Messrs Everett & Edgecumbe aircraft shed in a field at Colindale near Hendon. On 20 January, Grahame-White made three short flights from the field before returning to France in the first week in

February, having taken an option to purchase 207 acres of the pasture land between Colindale and Hendon for an aerodrome, ideally situated within easy reach of Watling Street (Edgware Road) and Hendon Station on the Midland Railway.

Not only had Grahame-White established a flying school in France and acquired an airfield in England within weeks of becoming a pilot but he had also decided to compete for the London *Daily Mail's* £10,000 prize, originally offered in 1906, for the first airman to fly from London to Manchester. For the attempt, Grahame-White purchased a Farman biplane for £1,500, in which he made his first flight from the Farman factory near Rheims on 14 March. The next day he took his mother up for her first flight! While at Rheims, he learned that George Holt Thomas, son of the founder of the *Daily Graphic*, also planned to enter a Farman biplane for the French airman, Louis Paulhan, in an attempt to win the £10,000. To be eligible for the *Daily Mail* prize, a pilot had to fly an aeroplane from a point within five miles of the newspaper's London offices to a point within five miles of its Manchester offices. As soon as Paulhan and Grahame-White gave notice of their separate attempts, the event developed into a race, much to the satisfaction of Lord Northcliffe and the public.

However, after the War Office refused Grahame-White permission to start his flight to Manchester from a military training ground at Wormwood

Claude Grahame-White photographed at Hendon in a Farman biplane on the eve of the London to Manchester attempt to win the £10,000 prize offered by the *Daily Mail*.

Scrubs, he made a hasty decision to take-off from the Royal Agricultural Society's abandoned showground at Park Royal near Ealing which was outside the five-mile limit. At dawn on 23 April Grahame-White took off in reasonable weather, but was later forced to abandon the attempt some 117 miles from London when his Farman was blown over and damaged in a storm after landing near Lichfield.

Meanwhile, Holt Thomas had chosen the fields at Hendon as Paulhan's take-off point for the race, although it too was outside the five-mile limit. The Frenchman's Farman had been assembled in Mr Everett's shed and was made ready for the attempt as Grahame-White's machine was being returned to London for urgent repairs. On the afternoon of 27 April, Paulhan left Hendon having sent Grahame-White a telegram advising him of his decision as they had agreed. However, for some reason the telegram was never delivered and by the time news of his departure reached Grahame-White, Paulhan was well on his way to Manchester and was to reach Lichfield before darkness fell.

After a hurried take-off, Grahame-White only managed to fly as far as the village of Roade, sixty miles from London, before the light grew too bad for him to continue. In an endeavour to overhaul his rival Grahame-White resorted to a 2.45am take-off in complete darkness. The *Daily Mail's* first air correspondent, Harry Harper, described the world's first aeroplane flight at night. 'I had the thrill, in a big steam-car, of guiding this first night-flying airman for several miles after his take-off, and while he was still groping his way through the darkness towards the lights of the nearest railway.' When Paulhan took-off later the same morning, he was only ten miles ahead of his rival, but being the more experienced pilot at that time, he managed to battle through high winds to reach Manchester first and claim the £10,000 prize. The contest had fired the imagination of the whole country, with supporters and officials hiring special trains to follow the progress of the aviators, and regular reports were sent to King Edward VII who was abroad at the time.

Blessed with good looks and charm, Grahame-White was the ideal person to become Britain's first aviation hero and despite being the gallant loser, soon became a household name. He promptly embarked on a hectic schedule of exhibition flights and air races up and down the country; there hardly seemed to be a day during the summer of 1910 when his airborne exploits were not making the headlines in newspapers and periodicals regardless of weather or conditions.

Meanwhile, enthusiasts gathered around the Hendon Aviation ground on Whit Monday 16 May had been treated to an impromptu air display, the first of many to be held on the site. Mr Everett continued in his unsuccessful attempts to become airborne in the 'Grass Hopper'. According to the local newspaper this was 'built on novel lines, embodying all the good points peculiar to both the Antoinette and Blériot types, and is considered by those qualified to judge to be in many respects superior to these types'. However, after running the full length of the field and back – a distance of over a mile – some eight or nine times, the machine still failed to become airborne. While the Everett was proving singularly inferior to the Antoinette and Blériot when it came to flying, a Mr A. Rawlinson brought his newly-acquired Henry Farman biplane to the field, and on Saturday evening, just after sunset, became the third aviator to take off successfully from Hendon. On the Whit Monday, the considerable crowds were rewarded by the sight of not only Everett and Rawlinson taxying around the field with varying degrees of success, but a large balloon from Alexandra Palace passed overhead. It is reported that the crowd 'pleasantly passed the afternoon away with songs, dancing and music'.

By July Grahame-White had sold his Blériot White Eagle to the Balloon Factory at Farnborough, forerunner of the Royal Aircraft Factory, and following his triumphant tour of the British Isles, during which he flew the first mail to be carried in an aeroplane between Blackpool and Southport, he accepted an offer of a considerable sum of money to appear at air meetings in the United States.

On 1 September, 1910, Grahame-White arrived in Boston accompanied by two mechanics, B.C. Hucks and R.H. Carr, a 100hp Gnôme-powered Blériot and the Farman. This was a tremendously successful venture. Between 6 and 12 September, he won a $2,000 prize offered by the Boston Globe by flying 33 miles cross-country in 40 minutes 6 seconds, to become the first English flyer to win a prize in America. At the same Boston meeting, Grahame-White also gained four other firsts, and three second, prizes to bring his total winnings for the week to £6,420. The British airman was considered to be a 'go-getter' by the Americans, and this trait combined with his English charm soon endeared him to American high-society, and New York's society ladies in particular. Indeed, his growing international reputation, as both a pilot and a showman, was considerably enhanced when he flew into Washington to pay President Taft a courtesy visit and landed the Farman in Executive Avenue outside the White House. However, the crowning climax of his visit to the United States came on 29 October when he won the Gordon Bennett international air race held at Belmont Park, New York, despite an objection from his American rival John Moisant. Grahame-White completed the 62.2 mile course in 1hr 1min 4.73secs to win the $10,000 first prize.

On his return to the British Isles in January 1911, Grahame-White moved his operation from Brooklands to Hendon where Horatio Barber's Aeronautical Syndicate, McArdle & Drexel and the Blériot School of Flying had taken residence. On 4 November, the School's chief flying instructor,

Pierre Prier, gave an exhibition of flying and four days later one of its pupils, J.G. Weir, later to become Controller of Aircraft Production in the Ministry of Munitions during the First World War, had the distinction of being the first Hendon trainee to qualify as a pilot.

Grahame-White attempted to float a company in partnership with Louis Blériot and Sir Henry Maxim, the British aviation pioneer who had built an unsuccessful steam-powered flying-machine in 1894 and also developed the machine-gun, to develop the Hendon site into an international aviation centre. The company's ambitious prospectus called for a share capital of £200,000 to be marketed in five shilling shares, a figure ridiculed by most of the Press at the time, with the exception of Northcliffe's newspapers, and consequently the issue failed with only £75,000 subscribed. The impatient Grahame-White promptly returned all subscriptions and formed the Grahame-White Aviation Company, investing his considerable American winnings in the venture with additional capital raised with the help of friends and relations, including his uncle Francis Willey and Sir Arthur du Cros, Chairman of the Dunlop Tyre Company, in order to take over the enterprise. The new company acquired a ten-year lease on Hendon's 207 acres, along with the right to purchase the freehold and additional acreage, and set about

One of the first aircraft to be built at Hendon was the innovative but commercially unsuccessful Valkyrie produced by Horatio Barber's Aeronautical Syndicate in 1911.

clearing, draining and levelling the pastures to form an aerodrome some two miles in circumference, Britain's third after Sheppey and Brooklands. His friend and co-director of the new company, Richard Gates, was appointed General Manager. The Grahame-White School of Flying was also established with Clement Grewswell as chief flying instructor, assisted by Charles Hubert, and a fee of 100 guineas, later reduced to seventy-five, was charged for a complete course of tuition. In addition, extra sheds were erected for the many new aviation companies wishing to set up shop at the new aerodrome.

One of the pilots who flew from Hendon during this period, and who was soon to rival Grahame-White as Britain's most dashing aviator, was Gustav Hamel. Despite his Germanic name, Hamel was the Eton-educated son of the Royal Physician, with a penchant for large powerful Mercedes motor-cars and flying. He was twenty-six years old when he learned to fly at the Blériot school at Pau in 1910 and his first flight of note occurred on 24 March 1911 when he flew from Hendon to Brooklands in a record fifty-eight minutes, after that his name was seldom out of the headlines.

However, the French were still dominating the aviation record books in Europe and on 12 April, Pierre Prier became the first to fly from London to Paris flying his 50hp Gnôme-powered Blériot from Hendon to Issy-les-Moulineaux in 3hr 56min. But apart from staging record-breaking flights, the main event of the year at Hendon aerodrome was undoubtedly the military demonstration given to the Parliamentary Aerial Defence Committee on 12 May. In front of the Duke and Duchess of Connaught and 120 Members of Parliament, who included the Prime Minister, H.H. Asquith, Lord Haldane, R. McKenna and Winston Churchill, several types of aeroplanes performed a series of military tasks. Farmans, Blériots, Barber's Valkyrie and Samuel F. Cody's *Flying Cathedral* gave an impressive demonstration of aerial scouting, dispatch carrying and 'bombing' from the air. The latter consisted of 100lb bags of flour aimed at circular targets marked out on the airfield and, what was to become a feature of later displays, a full size mock-up of a warship. Grahame-White took a number of MPs, including Balfour, Leader of the Opposition, for flights in his Farman and the following week was asked to address members of the committee at the House of Commons, all of which led to considerable interest but regrettably little action by the Government.

At the same time, in a further effort to stimulate the Government's interest in aviation, Horatio Barber presented four Valkyrie biplanes to the Admiralty but they were unfavourably received by naval pilots and were subsequently little used.

Less than a month later, Hendon was a compulsory landing point on the three-nation Circuit of Europe race that was won by the Frenchman, Jean Conneau.

He was again seen at Hendon in July en route to a narrow victory in the Circuit of Britain over his fellow countryman Jules Vedrines. An impromptu air display was later arranged at Hendon by Grahame-White as a benefit for Vedrines, who had won only a £200 consolation prize for his hard-fought second place in the Circuit of Britain race, while Conneau had received the full £10,000 *Daily Mail* prize. The benefit raised £2,000.

By this time several new companies were established at Hendon, one of which was the British Deperdussin Aeroplane Company founded by Lieutenant John Cyril Porte. Despite being recognised as an exceptional pilot having learnt to fly on a Demoiselle in 1910, Porte had recently been forced to retire from the Royal Navy due to ill-health. Lt Porte's company initially acted as agents for the French constructor, but when the Dutchman Frederick Koolhoven who, at the age of twenty-five had played a leading part in the design of the fast racing Deperdussins, was transferred to the British company as chief designer, it began to construct its own designs. A Deperdussin School of Flying was also established at Hendon as for a brief period was a Blackburn school.

In August, Grahame-White embarked on his second US tour during which he emulated his successes the previous year by winning most of the major prizes at the 1911 Boston meeting, flying the Farman and a 70hp Nieuport Monoplane. He also won several lucrative prizes at the Nassau Boulevard, New York meeting. Whilst he was in New York Grahame-White became engaged to a young socialite, Dorothy Taylor.

Although Grahame-White's Blériot had carried the first unofficial aerial post from Blackpool a year earlier, which incidentally was organised by fellow aviation pioneer and life-long business rival, George Holt Thomas, pilots of his flying school and those of the Blériot school were entrusted with carrying the first official mail to be carried by air when the Post Office inaugurated an aerial post between Hendon and Windsor to celebrate the coronation of King George V.

On Saturday 9 September, Gustav Hamel left Hendon at 4.58pm in a Blériot and aided by a strong tailwind, covered the twenty-one-mile route to Windsor in ten minutes, at a ground speed of over 100mph, to deliver a postcard to the Postmaster-General that he had written in flight. The service lasted until 29 September by which time Hamel and three other pilots had made twenty-one flights carrying more than 130,000 letters and postcards in thirty-nine bags with a total weight of 1,015lb. The net proceeds of the experiment amounted to £1,466.14s.10d. However, bad weather conditions had delayed several flights, and one of Grahame-White's instructors, Charles Hubert, crashed a Farman on his first take-off while carrying eight mail bags and broke both legs. On the insistence of his colleagues, he received £500 compensation from the

Gustav Hamel's Blériot leaving Hendon on 9 September 1911 carrying the first aerial post to Windsor to celebrate George V's coronation.

Post Office which considered the experiment 'of great public interest that would not be repeated for the time being'.

Meanwhile, yet more flying schools were opening for business at Hendon, namely those of W.H. Ewen, Scotland's most celebrated airman who had been the first to fly the Firth of Forth soon after gaining his

'ticket' with the Blériot School at Hendon, and J. Lawrence Hall, an aerial racing enthusiast.

The first of a long list of pilots, who would subsequently leave an indelible impression on British aviation, began their flying training at Hendon Aerodrome during 1911. Amongst those who joined the Grahame-White school were R. Bell Davies, who qualified for Royal Aero Club Certificate No 90, H. Biard and J.M. Salmond. George M. Dyott and W. Rhodes-Moorhouse attended the Blériot School of Flying while towards the end of the year, Hendon's first, and Britain's second, lady pilot, Mrs C. de Beauvois Stokes, qualified for Certificate No 153 at the Grahame-White School.

Hendon aerodrome was growing into a thriving business enterprise and when it was announced that the first full year's income amounted to more £11,000, £1,000 more than the figure projected in Grahame-White's original prospectus, which at the time seemed wildly optimistic, he had every right to feel that his decision to 'go it alone' had been vindicated.

The first flight of note from Hendon in 1912 was that of Henri Salmet, Pierre Prier's successor as chief pilot at the Blériot School of Flying, who flew to Paris in 3hr 25min on 7 March, thereby reducing his predecessor's time of the previous year by a full half hour.

Grahame-White continued his crusade to 'Wake Up England' to the exciting prospects for aviation, not only for sport, but as practical and reliable high-speed passenger transport and an essential component of the military services' armoury. In order to spread his message to as wide an audience as possible, he and his equally dedicated partner, Richard Gates, inaugurated weekly Saturday flying meetings at the London Aerodrome, Hendon.

Prominent flyers of the period were invited to take part in exhibition flights, speed handicaps and aerial races. Prizes and trophies were donated by several newspapers, such as Tit-Bits, and by many leading companies including Shell, Mappin & Webb and Rushmore Lamps as well as wealthy patrons of aviation, including the Maharajah of Alwar and Sir Thomas Lipton. The public was invited to take to the air in a Farman biplane with 'Wake Up England' painted on the nose and wings – two circuits for two guineas or special flights outside the aerodrome to Edgware and the Welsh Harp for five guineas. Passenger flights could also be booked any day, weather permitting, at the Aerodrome or from the offices of Messrs Keith Prowse. Various motoring events were organised on the ground and at each meeting a military band played a selection of popular tunes of the day.

A fully illustrated programme was on sale and a visitors' pavilion and restaurant were opened. Season tickets were also on offer, admitting holders to a properly-railed enclosure on all days when the aerodrome was open to the public – these tickets were priced at two guineas for 'Gentlemen' and £1.11s.6d for 'Ladies'. To ensure maximum coverage by the Press from home and abroad of the flying meetings, and any other events of interest held at the aerodrome, a full-time Press agent, Bernard Isaacs, was appointed and a permanent Press Club complete with bar was erected. The first meeting in

1912, on 5 April, attracted some 15,000 people through the turnstiles.

Another significant event in Hendon's development took place a few weeks later when George Holt Thomas took over the assets of Horatio Barber's Aeronautical Syndicate, and established the Aircraft Manufacturing Company, which came to be known as AIRCO. Early the previous year, Holt Thomas had acted as an agent for the War Office to purchase a Paulhan biplane and a Henry Farman Type III. He subsequently acquired a licence to produce Henry and Maurice Farman designs to be built by his new company at the London Aerodrome in sheds leased from the Grahame-White Aviation Co Ltd. This company also began to build aeroplanes, mostly biplanes based on Farman designs, but in order to produce designs of its own, an ex-Aeronautical Syndicate employee, twenty-year-old J.D. North, was hired in June as chief designer.

More than thirty sheds and hangars had sprung up along the western edge of the aerodrome by mid-1912, eleven of which belonged to Grahame-White while the rest were divided between the flying schools and various aviation companies such as Breguet Aeroplanes Ltd, Piggott Bros and R.O. Crawshay. Meanwhile, Hendon's fame was spreading to other parts of the country, especially in the West where Henri Salmet was making a tour to publicise the Blériot School of Flying. Indeed, on 18 May he made what was only the second crossing of the Bristol Channel in his Blériot XI. A week later, Grahame-White's mechanic, and later Blackburn's chief pilot, Bentfield Charles Hucks, flew the first airmail from Hendon to Bath in another Blériot, carrying letters from the Lord Mayor of London to his opposite number in Bath; the one hundred mile route was completed in 1hr 45min.

In the meantime, eighteen-year-old Dorothy Prentice had learned to fly on a Ewen flying school Blériot to become the country's youngest lady aviator, and the Hall school had taken delivery of one of the first Avro 500 trainers, developments of which would be closely associated with Hendon for nearly a quarter of a century.

In their quest to encourage a wider public to acquire the 'Hendon Habit', Grahame-White and Gates sought to create an event to rival the established social attractions of Cowes and Ascot. To this end, the first Aerial Derby was staged on 8 June 1912, sponsored by the *Daily Mail*. The course was a circuit of London over a distance of approximately eighty-one miles with six turning points at Kempton Park, Esher, Purley, Purfleet, Epping and High Barnet. More than 45,000 people gathered at the London Aerodrome to watch the seven starters flagged away at 4pm, the start having been delayed by bad weather. When all the competitors had left the Hendon area, the crowds were entertained with exhibition flights by Samuel

James Valentine's Bristol monoplane at Hendon prior to the first Aerial Derby held on 8 June 1912, in which he was placed fourth.

A Farman biplane turns around the airfield pylon during an air race at Hendon in 1912.

F. Cody in his 120hp Biplane, B.C. Hucks in a Nieuport Monoplane, and W.R. Raynham in an ABC-engined Wright biplane. The first competitor to land back at Hendon was T.O.M. Sopwith in his 70hp Blériot to complete the course in 1hr 23min 8sec. The Frenchman Guillaux in a Caudron seemed assured of second place but ran out of fuel almost within sight of the aerodrome leaving Gustav Hamel, carrying a lady passenger, Miss Trehawke Davis, in his Blériot to finish as runner-up. By the time W.B. Rhodes-Moorhouse brought his 50hp Radley-Moorhouse into third place, dusk was falling, so Grahame-White took off in a Farman fitted with two Rushmore searchlights in order to guide late finishers to the aerodrome. Although the stewards initially disqualified Sopwith for allegedly missing a turning point, his appeal against their decision was later upheld by the Royal Aero Club, and he was awarded the £250 first prize and a Gold Cup. The first Aerial Derby was considered a great success. It was estimated that the competitors' progress had been watched by half-a-million people around London, and it was destined to become a regular feature at Hendon for many years to come.

Two weeks later, Claude Grahame-White found time to marry Miss Dorothy Taylor at Chelmsford, with guests Sopwith and Hamel arriving at the reception by air, landing their Blériots on the lawns of the hotel.

Other meetings of note during 1912 included Ladies' Day held on 6 July, when Mrs Stokes won the major prize for the best flight of the day and also became the first lady pilot to fly with a lady passenger, Mrs Richard Gates.

On 26 September the 'First Illuminated Night Flying Display' proved to be one of the most popular events yet organised at the London Aerodrome. More than 10,000 lamps of varied colours and designs illuminated the enclosures while five aeroplanes took to the air outlined in electric lights and carrying powerful searchlights. They proceeded to 'bombard' a dummy warship, with the help of an excellent firework display by Joseph Wells & Sons, and the whole event was voted a resounding success by public and press alike. Two days later, a second military meeting was held featuring the latest RFC and RNAS machines, including a BE3 fitted with wireless, most of which had recently taken part in Army manoeuvres on Salisbury Plain.

A second night flying exhibition was planned for Guy Fawkes Night, but owing to inclement weather had to be postponed until 9 November. Again, vast crowds turned out on a frosty night to witness the destruction of the mock-up of a fort by Hendon's intrepid airmen. During the attack, Richard Gates suffered an engine failure, the resultant crash destroyed his Farman biplane 'Wake up England'. Gates escaped from the wreck with only minor injuries, but Grahame-White, who was known to have not a very high opinion of his manager's flying abilities, advised him to spend more of his valuable time on the ground than in the air in the future.

During 1912, some thirty fixtures attended by more than half a million paying spectators were held at the London Aerodrome making it another profitable year for the Grahame-White Aviation Company.

The same formula was adopted for the 1913 season but with additional meetings squeezed into the full calendar which stretched from February to November. Hendon was flourishing, as were no less than eight flying schools vying for business at the aerodrome – Beatty, Blackburn, Blériot, Deperdussin, Ewen, Grahame-White, Hall and Temple. Typical of the steady stream of aspiring young airman who made their way to Hendon was L.G. Hawker who gained his Royal Aero Club Certificate No 435 at the Deperdussin School of Flying on 4 March, and E. Bentley Beauman who made his first flight at the school a few days later.

Eight weeks and four flying hours later, Beauman took the flying test required to gain his certificate No 510 on 3 June. This consisted of two distance flights consisting of at least two miles each in five figures of eight, one altitude flight of at least 350ft and a landing with the engine cut within sixty yards of a special mark. A general fee of 75 guineas for a course of tuition was charged by all the schools; this amount could later be refunded by the War Office if the pilot

Claude Grahame-White in the cockpit of his Maurice Farman S.7 Longhorn on the airfield in 1913.

was accepted by the RFC or RNAS. Within days of gaining his ticket, Bentley Beauman was giving exhibition flights for the Deperdussin school, earning the princely fee of £10 a time. However, the aeroplane cost him £8 an hour to hire.

At the same time that Reginald Hugh Carr, Grahame-White's chief mechanic, was qualifying at his boss's school for Certificate No 504, a pupil of the Ewen school, Louis Strange, a nineteen-year-old son of a Dorset farmer, was being taught to fly in three weeks for a bet, by the Swiss, Edouard Baumann, recognised as one of the best of the pioneer instructors.

In the meantime, Hendon had become something of a mecca for baronets and gentleman-sportsmen. Sir Archibald Sinclair, Sir Bryan Leighton, and the motor-cycle racing son of a baronet, Sir Alastair Miller, who joined the Deperdussin School, and I.B. Hart-Davis, who had set a Land's End to John o'Groats record of 34hr 39min for the 886 miles in a 10hp Singer, all took their 'Tickets' at the London Aerodrome in 1913. So also did Christopher Draper, a pupil of the Grahame-White School who qualified for Certificate No 646 after 3hr 15min tuition from instructors Louis Noel and William Birchenough, the latter having learned to fly only three months earlier.

Nevertheless, not all of Hendon's commercial ventures prospered. On 23 August, Lt J.C. Porte announced the closure of his British Deperdussin Company following the failure of its latest aeroplane, the Seagull. Designed originally as a floatplane which the company had hoped would be purchased by the Admiralty, the Seagull was so underpowered that it was unable to take-off from water, and proved little better when tested at Hendon after being fitted with wheels.

However, others would take its place. Frederick Handley Page, who had been building experimental aeroplanes at Barking since 1909, moved into an old riding school in Cricklewood Broadway three years later to be close to the London Aerodrome where he rented a hangar. Flight testing of the Handley Page Type 'E' monoplane and Type 'G' biplane took place at Hendon during 1913 flown by E.R. Whitehouse and W. Rowland Ding respectively. In September, a Brooklands-based aircraft constructor, Noel Pemberton-Billing, wagered Frederick Handley Page £500 that he would be the first to get his ticket. After a series of hesitant hops at Hendon in his Type 'E' named the *Yellow Peril*, Handley Page conceded defeat to Pemberton-Billing who in fact gained his Certificate within a twenty-four hour period on 17/18 September!

The first Night Flying display of 1913 had been held on the evening of 13 June, again attracting vast crowds, much to the displeasure of the local inhabitants. The local newspaper reported that 'the ribald singing and chatter in the streets and the roar of the omnibuses as thousands of strangers passed up

The Grahame-White Baby, with Boxkites and Blériots in the background, at a 1913 Weekend Meeting.

and down the thoroughfares until nearly midnight was deafening'.

An even more 'enormous concourse of people' attended the August Bank Holiday meetings, but the highlight of London Aerodrome's busy season was the second Aerial Derby held on 20 September when the start and finish was seen by some 65,000 people. Gustav Hamel won the event, and a prize of £200 plus 100 guineas, in an 80hp Morane-Saulnier monoplane, completing the slightly revised 94.5 mile circuit of London course in 1hr 15min, at an average speed of 75.18mph. The next three places went to R.H. Barnwell in a Martinsyde, Harry Hawker in a Sopwith and W.R. Raynham in the prototype Avro 504 only two days after its first flight,

thus confirming the growing reliability of British planes.

Unfortunately, the day was somewhat marred when the Australian aviator, Sydney Pickles, took off at dusk with Mrs C. de Beauvois Stokes as his passenger, and crashed heavily on the aerodrome following an engine failure. Pickles escaped with minor injuries but Mrs Stokes was unconscious for three days and although she made a complete recovery, she never flew again. On the day following the Derby one of the competitors, the Frenchman, M. Debussy, was killed when his Breguet biplane crashed en route from Hendon to France.

A week later, the London Aerodrome hosted a third Naval and Military meeting during which

A Grahame-White Boxkite prepares to land on the airfield as the first spectators take their seats for another race meeting.

Marcus D. Manton took Lt Stellingwerf aloft in a Grahame-White biplane to test a Lewis gun fired from the air. On 2 October, a Grahame-White Type X *Charabanc* piloted by his chief pilot, Louis Noel, carried a record number of passengers, nine people with a combined weight of 1,371½lb, over Hendon for a twenty-minute flight. The same aeroplane was used by R.H. Carr who won the British Michelin Prize by covering 315 miles in a series of flights between Hendon and Brooklands on 6 November where incidently, a few days later, the Frenchman Adolphe Pégoud gave the first public exhibition of 'looping the loop' in England.

Naturally enough, Hendon was chosen as the venue for the first British pilot to attempt to emulate Pegoud's daring feat. On 26 November, B.C. Hucks looped a Blériot no less than six times, and promptly became the hero of London. In the meantime, G. Lee Temple and Gustav Hamel perfected the manoeuvre within days of Hucks' flight and looping displays soon became a popular feature of subsequent meetings at the London Aerodrome. To celebrate the event, Claude Grahame-White organised an 'Upside-Down' dinner for Hucks and Hamel at the Royal Aero Club during which, not only were the tables suspended from the ceiling but the menu was served back to front, beginning with coffee, followed by liqueurs and the loyal toast, then sweets, savoury, entree, fish and finally soup courses.

The last of fifty-one meetings to be held at the London Aerodrome during 1913 took place on 29 November. It was noteworthy for the public debuts of the Sopwith Tabloid flown by Harry Hawker, and the Willows-Hendon non-rigid airship. Although originally designed as a two-seater racing aeroplane, the Tabloid foreshadowed the mainstream of fighter development for many years to come. The airship, erected at Hendon by E.T. Willows, who made the first crossing of the English Channel in an airship, the Willows No 3, in 1910, was powered by a 60hp engine driving two unique swivelling airscrews which were designed by Frederick Handley Page.

Passenger flights in the airship were available at £5 for a stately circuit of the aerodrome, while airship pilot training was offered at a mere £100.

During 1913, more than a million people acquired the 'Hendon Habit'. The many and varied meetings had become the social events that Grahame-White and Gates had hoped they would, attracting the rich and famous including many show-business 'stars' of the day. Enrico Caruso, Robert Loraine, George Robey, Harry Tate and Ethel Levy were amongst the many personalities who made their first flights at Hendon.

Although his London Aerodrome flourished, Claude Grahame-White was disappointed at the British Government's apparent apathy towards aviation in general and military aviation in particular, despite the creation of the Royal Flying Corps in April 1912. He continued to direct his prodigious energy towards convincing the powers-that-be that active support of a British aviation industry was a matter of some urgency. To this end, he vigorously lobbied Members of Parliament, wrote a series of aeronautical books with the *Daily Mail* air correspondent, Harry Harper, and used the publicity generated by the Hendon displays when and wherever possible to pursue his cause.

One of his main allies in the campaign to 'Wake up England' to the future of aviation was Lord Northcliffe who in 1913 through his newspaper, the *Daily Mail*, offered £10,000 for the first aeroplane flight across the Atlantic. Grahame-White, Handley Page and Gustav Hamel immediately responded to the challenge by announcing their plans to win the prize for this, the most daunting of air voyages. Grahame-White's designers commenced work on a large seaplane, while Handley Page was commissioned to produce a twin-engined cabin biplane by a fifty-year-old English Lady married to a German Prince. Princess Anne Lowenstein-Wertheim, who had previously flown from Hendon to Paris and back in Handley Page's *Yellow Peril* with Rowland Ding, now put down a £1,000 deposit for the aeroplane in which she hoped to make her attempt.

After the failure of the British Deperdussin Company, J.C. Porte left for the United States following his selection as chief pilot for Glen Curtiss's Atlantic challenger, the twin-engined flying-boat *America*. In the meantime, Gustav Hamel had placed an order with the Martinsyde company, now resident at Brooklands, for a huge long-range monoplane which, although equipped with a watertight cabin, was unable to land on water.

Hamel, with his daring flying skills and dashing good looks, remained a firm favourite with the Hendon crowds, and on 2 January 1914 he took his good friend Miss Trehawke Davis aloft in her Blériot to experience a loop. Miss Davis thus became the first woman in the world to do so and three weeks later Lady Victoria Pery, daughter of Lord Limerick, became the second, again with Hamel in a Blériot at Hendon. In March, R.H. Carr looped a Grahame-White 'Lizzie', a machine designed for exhibition and aerobatic flying, to become the first British airman to loop a British aeroplane.

However, although aeroplanes were becoming more powerful and reliable, flying was still in its infancy and not yet a developed science. This was tragically brought home to the spectators when Gordon Lee Temple was killed in a crash at the London Aerodrome during a meeting on 27 January. Moreover, on 19 March, a benefit flying display was held for Marcel Dessoutter, a Grahame-White school instructor, who had lost a leg in an accident while flying a Blériot at a Saturday meeting the previous year. Most of the best-known aviators of the period took part in the benefit which raised nearly £2,000 for the young Frenchman. During his convalescence, he designed, and patented his own lightweight artificial leg and flew again just two months after his benefit. Before that, however, fellow Frenchman Philippe Marty would become the sixth aviator to lose his life at Hendon. Marty, who had first arrived at Hendon from France in 1913 delivering a brand new Caudron to the W.H. Ewen Aviation Co Ltd and subsequently stayed to become an instructor with the company's flying school, was killed during an aerobatic display in an 80hp Morane-Saulnier monoplane.

On the positive side, Hendon continued to be the showplace for all the latest innovations in aviation of the period. On 9 May the first parachute drop from an aeroplane over Great Britain was made by William Newell at Hendon from the Grahame-White *Charabanc* flown once again by R.H. Carr. Newell sat on the port undercarriage holding the 40lb parachute in his lap and was helped on his way as the aeroplane reached 2,000ft over the Edgware side of the aerodrome, by a kick from F.W. Gooden, himself an accomplished pilot of the day, who was seated on the lower wing. Newell made a safe landing in a field between Hendon and Mill Hill. Later, a local inventor and Blériot pilot, George Prensiel, demonstrated his revolutionary new parachute that was secured to the aviator in a cylinder and expelled by compressed air!

But only days later, Britain was mourning the loss of Gustav Hamel, the idol of the Hendon crowds, who disappeared on 23 May en route from Paris to Hendon. He had just collected a new 80hp Morane-Saulnier monoplane in which he planned to enter the third Aerial Derby. At this time of high international tension there was speculation that Hamel, son of a naturalised German, was the victim of a saboteur but as no trace of Hamel or his aeroplane were ever found, it remained speculation.

International tension remained high during the Whitsun weekend of 1914, when the country was plunged into a Zeppelin scare that resulted in severe

Farman's chief pilot, Pierre Verrier, taking part in the 1914 Whitsun meeting at Hendon flying a two-seat Maurice Farman S.11.

civil flying restrictions. However, Grahame-White had previously invited the French long-distance record breaker, Marcel Brindejonc des Moulinais, to take part in the Whit Sunday meeting at the London Aerodrome on 1 June. The intrepid Frenchman flew direct from Bremen in Germany to Hendon in an Etrich monoplane and promptly won the thirty mile cross-country Giesler Trophy Race. However, the Royal Aero Club refused to ratify his victory citing the fact that he had contravened the government's restrictions on overseas flights and should therefore be disqualified. Following a bitter dispute with Royal Aero Club officials, both Grahame-White and Richard Gates resigned from

A new 70hp Renault-powered Maurice Farman S.11 'Shorthorn' being prepared for the 1914 Aerial Derby.

The Avro Scout, a streamlined version of the 504, was an unsuccessful competitor in the 1914 Aerial Derby.

the Club and declared Brindejonc des Moulinais as the rightful winner.

Despite the loss of one of Britain's first flying heroes, the 1914 Aerial Derby held on 6 June attracted a record entry and a record number of spectators. More than 75,000 gathered at Hendon to watch the start and finish, amongst them, the first of many members of the British monarchy to visit the London Aerodrome, Queen Alexandra, the Queen Mother. The event was won by Walter L. Brock in an 80hp Morane-Saulnier at an average speed of 72.15mph to beat the likes of T.O.M. Sopwith, A.J. Alcock, L. Strange, R.H. Barnwell and R.H. Carr.

Winning the Aerial Derby started a remarkable spate of victories for the American Brock, who learned to fly with the Deperdussin School of Flying at Hendon, and his Morane-Saulnier. On 20 June he won the Hendon-Manchester-Hendon race, and on 11 July the Hendon-Paris-Hendon race. Brock also had the distinction of winning the last handicap race at Hendon at the 3 August meeting; this turned out to be the last aviation sporting event to be held in Britain before the outbreak of the First World War.

The following day Britain declared War on Germany and R. McKenna, Secretary of State at the

Roland Garros, who was to become France's first 'ace', seen landing in his Morane-Saulnier 'Parasol' during the Hendon–Paris–Hendon race held on 11 July 1914.

LEFT: The airfield at Hendon in 1910 showing the shed used by Louis Paulhan for his successful flight to Manchester to claim the *Daily Mail* prize.

FAR LEFT: An aerial view of Hendon during a 1912 race meeting showing the excellent spectator facilities, and the railway in the background.

BELOW: On 2 October 1913 Grahame-White's chief pilot, Louis Noel, carried a record nine passengers, including Reginald Carr on the extreme right, aloft from Hendon in the G-W Type X 'Charabanc'.

Hendon, 2nd oct. 1913

Yours very sincerely

Louis Noël

A souvenir of my world's record on the aero Char-a-banc (120 H.P. Austro Daimler) for carrying nine passengers weighing 1,371½ lbs ...

Home Office and one of the MPs who attended the first Military Flying demonstration at Hendon in May 1911, issued an order prohibiting the flying of any aeroplanes over the whole of the United Kingdom except Naval or Military aircraft or those flying under Naval or Military orders.

In the period between March 1910 to August 1914, a total of 863 people learnt to fly in England, qualifying for the Royal Aero Club Certificate. Of that total, 185 learnt at Hendon where, at one time or the other, eleven different schools of flying had operated. The most successful of these were the Grahame-White with seventy-one, the Ewen, later the British Caudron Co Ltd, with thirty-eight, Blériot with thirty-five and the Deperdussin with twenty-four; many of these airmen were to play an important part in developing the art of aerial warfare during the next four years.

Gustav Hamel's Blériot XI in front of the crowds at one of the fifty-one meetings held at Hendon in 1913.

2 DEFENCE OF THE REALM

HENDON AT WAR

On 4 August 1914 Captain Murray Frazer Sueter RN, head of the Admiralty's Air Department, wrote to Grahame-White stating that he was commandeering the London Aerodrome under the Defence of the Realm Act. Thus Hendon became a Royal Naval Air Station. The very next day Claude Grahame-White sent the first of many lengthy letters to Winston Churchill, First Lord of the Admiralty, stating that he would be prepared to do whatever was necessary for the War effort and requesting contracts for the production of aircraft for the RNAS.

Churchill had already circulated a memo to members of the government referring to the defence of London from Zeppelin raids which stated that: 'A squadron of aeroplanes will be established at Hendon in close telephonic communications with other stations, for the purpose of attacking enemy aircraft which may attempt to molest London. It is indispensable that airmen of the Hendon flight should be able to fly by night, and their machines must be fitted with the necessary lights and instruments'.

By 7 August the RNAS had established at Hendon a Defence of London Flight, and an aircraft acceptance park for the inspection of aircraft delivered by the manufacturers at Hendon commanded by ex-British Deperdussin Company boss, J.C. Porte, with the rank of Squadron Commander. He chose as his second in command, an ex-Deperdussin pupil and instructor, E. Bentley Beauman, now a Flight Sub-Lieutenant in the RNAS. Beauman was detailed to pick-up a Caudron, the Flight's only aeroplane, from Eastleigh and fly it direct to Hendon which he managed to do despite never having flown the type before. The unit's only other equipment was a 500ft captive balloon that Sub-Lt Beauman flew on occasions from the Battersea balloon grounds to check the effectiveness of London's blackout. Within a short period of time Porte successfully re-activated a 100hp Deperdussin that had laid in storage on the aerodrome since the closure of his company and he used it to carry out the flight's first inconclusive patrol on 5 September.

In the meantime, the fledgling RFC had assembled a total of thirty-seven assorted aeroplanes at Dover ready to fly to France. This force, comprising the British Expeditionary Force air component, crossed the channel on 14 August and included a number of Hendon-trained pilots, Major John Salmond and

Grahame-White staff salvaging parts of aeroplanes from the collapsed hangars after a gale in the spring of 1917. The tailplane, wheel and propeller are all that remained of a Grahame-White Type XV, No 8785, ordered by the RFC in 1916.

Amongst many Grahame-White aeroplanes destroyed when hangars collapsed in the gale were these two Grahame-White school type XV trainers, Nos 303 and 311.

Lieutenant Louis Strange amongst them. Grahame-White's chief pilot, Louis Noel, also crossed the Channel to become one of France's early aces.

Another result of the Defence of the Realm Act (DORA) was that all Hendon's remaining civilian flying schools were contracted to train pilots for the RNAS and Royal Flying Corps alongside their civilian pupils. In September, two young RNAS officers of note, Reginald Alexander Warneford and Gerald Edward Livock, began their training with the Grahame-White school under the watchful eye of two famous pre-war instructors, Marcus D. Manton and Warren Merriam. Grahame-White continued to send the Admiralty advice on how to wage the war with numerous proposals for schemes such as the use of barges moored in the North Sea to act as stepping stones for aeroplanes en route to drop bombs on Germany. Furthermore, on 25 August he wrote the following letter to the First Sea Lord:

Dear Mr Churchill,

Being anxious to be given scope for my initiative and organising ability and in view of the fact that I was the first Englishman to qualify for an aviator's certificate, have over five years experience in the instruction, maintenance and in fact every branch of the aviation industry in addition to being a practical flyer of every type and build of aeroplane, may I ask you to be kind enough to raise my appointment to that of Flight Commander.

You can rest assured I shall use my best endeavours to prove of service to the country.

Yours very truly

Claude Grahame-White

Within days this was granted and on the evening of 5 September, Flight Commander Grahame-White with Flight Lieutenant Richard Gates, also newly-commissioned, acting as observer armed with a rifle, took off in a Henry Farman biplane on the first defensive night sortie of the War. No contact was made with the enemy. Other flights followed in response to further false alarms, one of which resulted in the unfortunate death of Richard Gates. He took off alone at 10.30pm on 10 September in response to an alert from the Admiralty, in spite of being forbidden to fly at night by Grahame-White following an earlier crash landing. He again crashed heavily while attempting to land back at Hendon and subsequently died of his injuries. Gates was the first British aviator to lose his life in the cause of aerial defence of Great Britain during the war.

The death of his friend and partner who had contributed so much to stimulate the advance of British aviation, had a profound effect on Grahame-White and ultimately hastened the demise of the London Aerodrome that they had both worked so long and hard for.

Nevertheless, the Grahame-White Aviation Company received its first wartime contract from the Admiralty for twenty-four BE2c aircraft on 29

September; this was followed by an order for twelve Grahame-White Type XV, known as Type 1600 in the RNAS, a month later. Other RNAS contracts placed with Hendon-based factories included twelve Caudron GIVs with the British Caudron Company, now managed by A.M. Ramsay following the departure of W.H. Ewen who had joined the RFC, while the Aircraft Manufacturing Company (AIRCO) was producing Maurice Farman S7 'Longhorn' and S11 'Shorthorn' trainers under licence for the Royal Flying Corps, having acquired additional workshops on the Edgware Road near Colindale Road within a mile of the aerodrome.

At the end of October, Naval aircraft stationed at Hendon included two Avro 500s, one Caudron GIII, a Maurice Farman, two Henry Farmans, one Deperdussin and a Handley Page Type 'G'. Other RNAS aircraft with a strong Hendon connection were the Blériot which Miss Trehawke Davis presented to the Navy, to be numbered 903, on the outbreak of war, and the Willows IV airship which later served as a prototype for more than a hundred S.S (Submarine Scout) type airships built during the war. However, apparently neither aircraft operated from the Station.

Meanwhile, Grahame-White, frustrated at not being given what he considered to be a proper job, made himself unpopular both with his Admiralty superiors and his Commanding Officer. Early in 1915 he wrote yet another letter to Churchill demanding to know why Captain Sueter had ignored his scheme for a seaplane raid on the Kiel Canal, and criticising the efficiency of the Defence of London Flight and therefore the competence of Sqn Cdr Porte. To make matters worse, Grahame-White also wrote an article expressing his views on military aviation which was published in the magazine *War Illustrated* on 30 January 1915. This article led to him being accused of contravening Article 14 of King's Regulations & Admiralty Instructions which stated that 'All persons belonging to the fleet are forbidden to write for publications, or to publish or cause to be published, either directly or indirectly, any matter or information relating to the naval service unless permission of the Admiralty has been first obtained.' In his defence, Grahame-White maintained that he had not been aware that he was infringing the King's Regulations; that there was nothing in the article that was not to be found in the daily press; and that he had a contract with the magazine that he was obliged to honour. The matter was finally dropped with a directive from Porte that if he wished to publish anything in the future, a copy of the text should be forwarded to the Admiralty for its approval.

On 12 February, Grahame-White was able to take part in the first RNAS raids directed against German bases on the Belgium coast. Piloting an 80hp Gnôme-powered Henry Farman F20, he crossed the Channel to within four miles of Nieuport, only to be forced down into the sea by a snowstorm. Fortunately, his flight had been observed by a French minesweeper which picked him up and transferred him to a British gunboat. Upon his return to England he learned that he was to be posted to command an armoured train in France. He promptly resigned his commission in order to concentrate on expanding his aircraft factory.

Apart from being the base for the Defence of London Flight, an RNAS aircraft acceptance park, and extremely busy flying training centre, many aspiring aircraft manufacturers brought their prototype machines to Hendon to attempt their maiden flights and so compete with the resident manufacturers for lucrative military contracts that were in the offing.

One such hopeful was the Mann & Grimmer M1, a two-seat fighter-reconnaissance biplane powered by a 100hp Anzani engine which drove two-chain-driven propellers. Financed by W.H. Bonham-Carter MP and designed by seventeen-year-old R.F. Mann and his ex-schoolmaster, R.P. Grimmer, the M1 was built at Surbiton in component form and assembled at Hendon where it made a hesitant first flight on 19 February with W. Rowland Ding at the controls. Later in the year Ding made a crash landing at the aerodrome following a gearbox seizure. Although he escaped injury, the M1 was severely damaged and Bonham-Carter withdrew his support for the project soon after.

Another was the Pemberton-Billing PB9 which was designed and flown at Brooklands by Lt Cdr Noel Pemberton-Billing who had planned the RNAS attack on Zeppelin sheds at Friedrichshafen on 21 November 1914, which was led, incidentally, by a regular participant at pre-war Hendon meetings, Flight Lieutenant S.V. Sippe. Following testing at Hendon, the PB9 was requisitioned by the RNAS as a training aircraft (No 1297) while his later design, the PB23 pusher biplane fighter, made its first flight from the aerodrome in September. However, the most significant aircraft to make its maiden flight at Hendon during 1915 was the AIRCO DH1 designed by Geoffrey de Havilland who had joined AIRCO from the Royal Aircraft Factory in June 1914. At the outbreak of war, de Havilland, an RFC reservist, at once joined up and flew a Blériot on submarine reconnaissance, reaching the rank of Captain before resuming his position at AIRCO. The DH1, a single-seat reconnaissance biplane with a pusher-engine layout, was given its first flight by de Havilland in January 1915. The successful pusher-layout was retained for his second AIRCO design, the DH2, which was to become the first single-seat fighter to be built in quantity for the RFC.

By 1915, casualties in the air war over Europe were mounting at an alarming rate and on 26 April two Hendon-trained pilots died on the Western Front. 2nd Lieutenant Frederick William Polehampton was shot down over Ypres only seven months after graduating from the Grahame-White school. On the same day less than twenty miles away, Lieutenant W.B. Rhodes Moorhouse, the charismatic sportsman pilot and racing driver of pre-war Hendon, succumbed to injuries received during a low-level attack on Courtrai railway station. For his gallantry, he was posthumously awarded the first Victoria Cross of the war. On the night of 6/7 June, Flight Sub-Lieutenant R.A.J. Warneford of No 1 Squadron RNAS flying a Morane-Saulnier Parasol from Dunkirk, intercepted and destroyed Zeppelin LZ37 near Ghent, the first airship to be bought down by air attack. For this deed, Warneford became the RNAS's first VC holder but only twelve days later he was to die in a flying accident. Hendon's 'third' Victoria Cross was awarded to Major Lanoe George Hawker on 24 August 'for success in Air Combat'. He had forced down three enemy aircraft in one day while flying a Bristol Scout.

Meanwhile, casualties were also mounting in the air war on the home front. On the night of 31 May, a Sopwith Gun Bus belonging to the London Defence Flight, took off from Hendon in response to a genuine Zeppelin alert. Unfortunately the aircraft crashed while attempting to land in darkness near Hatfield, killing the pilot, Flt Lt Barnes RNAS, and injuring the gunner, Flt Sub-Lt Ben Travers, who was later to make his name as a West End playwright. In addition to being a major acceptance park for British-built aircraft, miscellaneous French

and American machines purchased by the RNAS began to arrive at Hendon during 1915. Many were obscure and untried designs that were never used operationally, such as the American Burgess Gunbus, built by a company later acquired by Curtiss, and the Thomas T2 scout, constructed in the USA by two English brothers who previously worked for the Sopwith company. A considerable quantity of Curtiss JN3/4 Jennies, ordered on the recommendation of J.C. Porte who virtually became Curtiss's agent in Britain, were later used as advanced trainers.

The majority of those undergoing training with the five schools of flying still operating at Hendon by the end of the year were destined for the services, with one or two notable exceptions. The resident schools used several types of primitive training machines such as the Henry Farman derivatives favoured by the Grahame-White and Hall schools while 50hp Gnome-powered developments of the Wright biplane were used by the Beatty-Wright School of Flying formed by an American, G.W. Beatty. These three schools constructed and repaired their own aircraft. The London & Provincial Aviation Company, recently established by Henry Slive MP, and the Ruffy-Baumann School of Flying were equipped with the more advanced Caudron GIII biplane.

The Ruffy-Baumann School was considered as one of the most professional, having been established at

Sub-Lieutenant Reginald Alexander Warneford was an early pupil of the Grahame-White school at Hendon. He qualified in December 1915 and less than six months later was awarded the first RNAS Victoria Cross.

H.H. Balfour, later Lord Balfour of Inchrye, seen in front of a Ruffy-Baumann school Caudron GIII at Hendon in July 1915.

Hendon by the Swiss ex-Ewen and Beatty instructor, Edouard Baumann, in partnership with his brother and an Italian, G. Ruffy. Amongst those who enrolled at the School during 1915 were H.H. Balfour, later Lord Balfour of Inchrye, and Albert Ball who gained his ticket, No 1898, on 15 October. Ball was considered by his instructor as a slow learner who managed to crash his Caudron on only his third lesson. One of more than forty Belgians who learned to fly at Hendon during the War, Willy Coppens, qualified for the RAe Club Certificate No 2140 on the 9 December after thirty lessons and 3hr 56min in the air with the Ruffy-Baumann school during which time he learned, on his own admission, 'little about flying'. At the same time, his fellow countryman Andre de Meulemeester was attending the Grahame-White school. By the end of the war, these two fellow countrymen were to become Belgium's highest-scoring aces with thirty-seven and eleven victories respectively.

Other Hendon graduates included the Australian Roderic Dallas, New Zealander Alfred de Bathe Brandon and Englishmen Leonard H. Rochford and Gwilyn H. Lewis. While Lewis was under training with the London & Provincial school, his fifty-year-old father enrolled with the Grahame-White school in order to 'find out what this flying thing was all about'. Earlier in the year, one of Canada's leading air pioneers, Theodore C. Macauley had spent some time at Hendon. In May 1915, Macauley had flown Canada's first passenger service from Toronto to Halifax and back in a Curtiss flying-boat *Sunfish*, and a year later arrived in England intending to join the RFC. However this was not to be and he returned to Canada where he resumed his record-breaking long distance flights before disappearing during a flight along the St Lawrence the following year.

In the summer months flying training started as early as 5am in order to take advantage of the calm air at that time of day. Students congregated in the pilot's room, the old London Aerodrome Press Club, to await the opportunity of going aloft — weather permitting. Clipped-wing Blériots, dubbed 'Penguins', were used for high-speed taxying without leaving the ground. Pupils were taught the rudiments of flying by instructors of many nationalities, shouting instructions over their shoulders. Those flying solo were guided by series of elaborate, and often confusing, hand signals from the ground. Despite the fact that there were often as many as a dozen training machines more or less in the air at any one time, few serious injuries resulted from the numerous crashes that occurred, usually resulting in the destruction of the fragile biplanes. There was at the time no air traffic control and only a few of the schools had a gentleman's agreement to fly training circuits in any particular direction, the Grahame-White school flew anti-clockwise while the Beatty flew clockwise. The others flew wherever there was a clear space and near-misses between inexperienced pilots in underpowered machines, were not uncommon. One of the reasons for Hendon's popularity as a venue for fledgling fighter pilots was its proximity to London. The bright lights of the West End were only a bus or tram ride away from the aerodrome whenever bad weather, or broken aircraft, interrupted flying training.

Even during the war years, several record-breaking attempts were made at Hendon such as when Harry Hawker reached a height of 18,393ft in a Sopwith Tabloid over the aerodrome on 6 June to create a new British altitude record. In this first full year of the war, aircraft manufacturers, many of which had worked out of lock-up garages and converted stables only months earlier, had moved to purpose-built new factories and were grappling with the complexities of mass-producing modern warplanes. In addition to Farman trainers, the first DH2 fighter scouts destined for the RFC were starting to leave AIRCO's Hyde factory for flight testing at Hendon, and in December the prototype of the world's first heavy bomber was assembled at the aerodrome for its maiden flight.

With typical foresight, Capt Murray Sueter had recognised the value of such an aircraft for coastal defence at an early stage of the war and placed an order for one machine with the small Handley Page Aircraft Company. On the evening of 9 December the massive prototype Handley Page 0/100 was manhandled along Edgware Road and Colindale Avenue from the Cricklewood factory to Hendon aerodrome by a squad of sailors, company employees, and Frederick Handley Page who supervised the removal of tram wires, lamp posts and overhanging tree branches. The $1\frac{1}{2}$ mile journey took five hours. On 17 December, the giant biplane with 100ft wingspan, powered by two 250hp Eagles, Rolls-Royce's first aero-engine, made a successful maiden flight with Lieutenant-Commanders E.W. Stedman, pilot, and J.T. Babington, co-pilot at the controls.

Grahame-White, in the meantime, had commenced construction of new workshops and increased his workforce from twenty, at the outbreak of war, to more than one thousand. In response to an Admiralty competition for aeroplanes expressly designed for bombing, the Company had produced a large single-engine biplane, the Type 18, but it was judged inferior to the Short Bomber which subsequently went into production for the RNAS.

In order to justify the heavy expenditure of expansion, Grahame-White again wrote to Churchill, following the latter's visit to the Defence of London Flight at Hendon on 17 April, requesting additional orders for 100 aeroplanes. The Admiralty's reaction was less than encouraging. It complained of the company's late deliveries of existing orders and wrote 'it does not appear to Mr Churchill to be a practical proposition to place further orders until better progress has been made with the machines now under construction.' The

Geoffrey de Havilland's first design for AIRCO, the DH1, forerunner of the RFC's successful DH2 fighter, made its maiden flight at Hendon in July 1915.

fact of the matter was that whereas hopelessly optimistic delivery dates were being promised by other companies seeking contracts, Grahame-White had from the outset forecast that his factory would not make its first deliveries until early 1916; although production of the BE2s and Farmans was on schedule for that date, the Admiralty remained as yet, unconvinced.

On 1 January 1916, the War Office announced that Captain Richard Bell Davies, RNAS, had been awarded the Victoria Cross for his courageous rescue, whilst flying a single-seat Nieuport in the

Dardanelles, of a fellow pilot who had been forced down in enemy territory. Davies was the fourth Hendon-trained pilot to be so honoured. At the end of the month, two BE2cs, an RNAS machine and one belonging to a detachment of No 17 Reserve Aircraft Squadron RFC, took off from Hendon to intercept a night raid by nine German Navy Zeppelins, but no contact was made with the enemy.

By 16 February the RFC's 18th Wing had taken over responsibility for the capital's defence from the RNAS and a detachment of No 19 Reserve Aircraft

Squadron (RAS), headquartered at Hounslow and equipped with BE2cs, was deployed at Hendon. It was an ex-Hendon pupil, 2nd Lt de Bathe Brandon RFC, who was credited with the destruction of Zeppelin LZ15 on the night of 31 March, flying a BE2c of 19 RAS detachment at Hainault Farm. After attacking the airship with machine-gun and incendiary bombs over Purfleet, Surrey, LZ15 eventually came down in the sea off Westgate, Kent, and its crew was captured. On 3 April, 2nd Lt de Bathe Brandon was awarded the Military Cross for his exploit.

Despite the disbandment of the RNAS Defence of London Flight, Hendon remained a Royal Naval Air Station under the command of Flight Commander C. Hornby who had replaced Flt Cdr J.C. Porte at the beginning of the year. Porte had been posted to Felixstowe to supervise the arrival of the first of more than 100 American Curtiss H type flying-boats ordered by the RNAS, eight of which were assembled at AIRCO. The Curtiss H-4 had been developed from the *America* flying-boat in which Porte had planned an Atlantic crossing before the outbreak of war delayed the attempt. Another aviation pioneer who played an important part in shaping the RNAS's offensive strategy during the early part of the war was Noel Pemberton-Billing who, having resigned his commission, was elected as Member of Parliament for Hertford in March of 1916. At the same time, he sold his interests in

Pemberton-Billing Ltd after his advanced PB25 fighter failed to attract substantial orders from the War Office. Shortly after the sale, the name of the company was changed to that of the Supermarine Aviation Works Ltd.

Captain Henri Biard, who would later make his name as a Supermarine test pilot, had returned to Hendon after a spell with the Central Flying School to take up a temporary position as an instructor with Grahame-White's school. During this period Biard took George Bernard Shaw aloft for his first flight in an aeroplane. Shaw was just one of many personalities who continued to visit the aerodrome during the war years. Indeed, if the weather was reasonable, actresses and showgirls from the West End were often taken for a flight by Claude Grahame-White in his *Charabanc*. One of his most frequent visitors was Miss Ethel Levy, a popular musical comedy actress of the time and this period coincided with the gradual breakdown of his marriage to Dorothy, only one of the many problems that contributed to Grahame-White's subsequent nervous breakdown.

He had completed the construction of his new factory, with financial assistance from his old benefactor, his uncle Francis Willey, and the first BE2c of the War Office contract was delivered in March as predicted, although production had been constantly beset with bureaucratic problems caused in the main by inexperienced Admiralty inspectors

The Dyott Battleplane, a gigantic 'fighter' armed with a two-pounder Vickers cannon, took to the air for the first time on 25 April 1915. It did not attract any orders.

The Grahame-White company produced several unsuccessful experimental designs during the early years of the war including this two-seat 'Twin Airscrew Experimental Project' in 1916. It was destined never to fly.

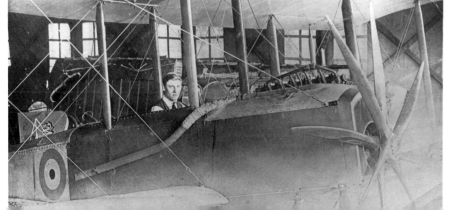

and the incorporation of a myriad of modifications. Following the completion of ten Breguet BM5 bombers for the RNAS, known as the Grahame-White Type 19, the company built a single-seat scout prototype, the Type 20, in an effort to stimulate further production. The aeroplane, powered by an 80hp Clerget rotary engine, virtually a biplane development of the Morane-Saulnier Type G monoplane, was not a success.

Other less than practical machines that made their first flights at Hendon during the year included the Dyott Battleplane. The huge biplane, powered by two 120hp Beardmore engines and fitted with a massive Vickers two-pounder Mk IV gun, made its maiden flight on 25 April flown by the co-designer, George M. Dyott. A rare failure from the drawing board of Geoffrey de Havilland, however, was the AIRCO DH3, a similarly powered twin-engined bomber that first flew in June. A much more successful design from the same stable took to the air at Hendon two months later, again with de Havilland at the controls. The DH4 was the first aircraft designed from the outset as a day-bomber to be ordered in quantity for RFC.

41

It was in August 1916 that the War Office took over the various civilian schools on the aerodrome and grouped them all together as the Royal Flying Corps Civilian School of Instruction, Hendon. Despite the title, purely civilian training was effectively brought to an end by its formation, while the steady stream of military personnel posted to Hendon continued unabated. The year also saw the arrival of a contingent of trainees from one of Britain's oldest allies, Portugal, while one of the first entries assigned to the redesignated RFC school was Lt Edward 'Mick' Mannock. Mannock gained his Pilot's Certificate on 28 November despite suffering from a serious astigmatism in the left eye. A week earlier, while flying a DH2 over the Somme, Major Lanoe Hawker VC was shot down and killed by Manfred von Richthofen.

On 5 October, George Holt Thomas formed Aircraft Transport and Travel Ltd. The third year of a European war, during which all international civil flights were banned, may have seemed an

Marcus D. Manton, one of Grahame-White's most distinguished pre-war and wartime instructors, in the cockpit of a Grahame-White Type XV.

A production AIRCO DH4 in front of Hendon's original control tower. A7995 was one of a contract for 689 DH4s built at Colindale and flight-tested at Hendon during 1916/17.

inappropriate time to establish Britain's first airline, but inspired by the recent flight of a Handley Page 0/100 carrying twenty passengers to 7,000ft over Hendon, Holt Thomas was determined to be in a position to operate commercial passenger flights as soon as hostilities ceased.

Meanwhile, after spending six weeks in hospital following his nervous breakdown, Grahame-White's persistence was rewarded with a War Office contract for 600 Avro 504J/K training biplanes.

In November, the prototype DH5 'staggerwing' fighter was test-flown by B.C. 'Benny' Hucks and a total of 549 were ordered from AIRCO and the British Caudron Company, which to date had produced small numbers of Caudron GIII and GIV trainers. On 11 November, yet more diverse US

types were accepted for official trials at RNAS Hendon. These included the twin-engined Curtiss Canada (No 3448), a development of the JN-4Can Jenny built at the company's plant in Canada, and the single-seat single-engine R-2 heavy bomber built by the Burgess Company, another enlarged development of the ubiquitous JN-2 Jenny. Both were rejected by the RNAS trials pilots despite 100 of each having been ordered by the Admiralty before the trials were conducted. The same fate befell the 135hp Hall Scott-powered Sloane-Day HI biplane (No 3701).

At this time the aircraft that was destined to be built at Hendon in larger numbers than any other type, the DH6 trainer, made its first flight. A total of 600 machines were ordered, virtually off the drawing board, from AIRCO and on 13 January 1917, 750 from the Grahame-White Company.

At the beginning of December, Claude Grahame-White had divorced his wife and two weeks later married the actress, Ethel Levy. With a new marriage and substantial Government contracts, future prospects seemed better for him than at any time since the outbreak of the War.

Another one-off design that was extensively flight-tested at Hendon was the Nestler Scout, a compact fighter-scout designed by the Frenchman, E. Boudot, for the company of portable hangar manufacturers. Ironically on 26 March, the Nestler Scout crashed into one of the London & Provincial hangars during a demonstration of its aerobatic qualities. The aircraft was destroyed and the pilot, J.B. Fitzsimmons, killed in the accident. Soon after this unfortunate event, a new Grahame-White single-seat scout, the Type 21, made its first flight but with the factory now heavily committed to the production of Avro 504s and DH6s, development of this aircraft was not proceeded with.

On 21 April, Squadron Commander F.G. Brodribb took over command of RNAS Hendon from Flt Cdr Hornby with the Station continuing in its role as a test centre of not only new aircraft types but of experimental equipment such as the Waygood-Otis compressed-air catapult designed by R.F. Carey. Over a series of tests carried out during October 1917, Flight Commander R.R. Perry RNAS became the first pilot to be successfully launched from the

Part of a Grahame-White assembly shop at Hendon showing in the foreground three Type XV trainers and in the background several DH6 trainers, part of an order for two hundred, in various states of production.

The Royal Flying Corps mock-Tudor Mess was built at Hendon during the summer of 1917.

seven confirmed victories, was Britain's highest-scoring fighter pilot at the time of his death. On 3 June he was awarded a posthumous Victoria Cross.

The German High Command also stepped-up air raids on London and other targets in Britain using the new Gotha GV heavy bomber which was replacing the increasingly vulnerable Zeppelin. The first daylight raid over London by the new aircraft on 5 June caught the Home Defence squadrons unawares. No 19 RAS at Hendon could only put up three aircraft, a DH4, a DH5 and an Armstrong Whitworth FK8 'Big Ack', none of which made contact with the enemy. Although the Air Board had decreed that DH4s should replace the various obsolete types that equipped most Reserve Aircraft Squadrons, deliveries were slow; in face of the Gotha threat aircraft had to be withdrawn from the Western Front. A month later, five DH4s, which had three times the rate of climb of a BE2c, took off from Hendon to intercept a heavy Gotha raid. Although none of the raiders, which killed 93 and injured 193, were bought down by the defending forces, resistance was such that the Gothas reverted to night raids.

During the summer of 1917, the Royal Flying Corps embarked on an extensive expansion programme at Hendon that included the creation of No 2 Aircraft Acceptance Park, incorporating the RNAS delivery and distribution centre, and the building of an impressive mock-Tudor Officers' Mess on the south of the aerodrome.

catapult in an Avro 504. Two Sopwith Pups also took part in the trials at Hendon but by the end of the year the entire project, which was way ahead of its time, moved to a converted barge moored off the Isle of Grain in the Thames estuary.

In the early months of 1917, British casualties in the air mounted alarmingly, and in 'Bloody' April the RFC alone lost almost a third of its aircraft on the Western Front. The bad news was made worse with the death of Captain Albert Ball whose SE5 crashed near Arras in mysterious circumstances on the evening of 7 May. Twenty-year-old Ball, with forty-

As the expansion of aircraft factories on and around Hendon also proceeded apace, a spur line from the Midland Railway was built around the aerodrome boundary from Silk Stream junction to the southeast of the airfield to the AIRCO factory at Edgware Road, and German prisoners-of-war built Aerodrome Road linking Colindale Road with the Watford Way. The PoWs were camped in fields to the north of the aerodrome, where, it was rumoured, they would act as a deterrent to German air raids on the aerodrome, but it was more likely that No 19 RAS and an anti-aircraft gun battery situated in Mill Hill Broadway, were more effective deterrents.

In spite of the threat of bombing, aircraft manufacturers continued to gravitate to Hendon's boundaries. Amongst them was the British Nieuport and General Aircraft Co Ltd which produced French Nieuport designs under licence at Cricklewood, but was beginning to develop its own types, designed by H.P. Folland. Another, the British Aerial Transport Co Ltd (BAT), was formed in June 1917 by Lord Waring, of Waring & Gillow, a company which was already a major Government aircraft sub-contractor. The ex-Deperdussin designer, Frederick Koolhoven, who left Armstrong Whitworth to become chief designer of the new company, renewed his connection with Hendon by using a hangar in the southwest corner of the aerodrome to assemble machines that were constructed in the BAT workshops at Willesden.

A production AIRCO DH5 staggerwing fighter, the prototype of which was flown for the first time by B.C. 'Benny' Hucks from Hendon in November 1916.

However, all was not well with the DH6 trainer, large quantities of which had been ordered from Hendon factories. Designed from the outset as an easily built training aircraft, it was proving to be anything but easy to produce. In order to cope with the DH6 contract, which would soon lead to a series of prolonged and bitter disputes with the War Office, Grahame-White continued his expansion at Hendon with financial backing from the Government which advanced him a total of £320,000. After supplies from the USA dried up in April, the specifications of the contract called for the use of timber which a laboratory report, commissioned by Grahame-White, described as unsuitable. When his own warnings about the consequences of building aircraft from sub-standard materials were ignored, he complied.

However, following several fatal accidents to early production machines, the Air Board immediately stopped all production of DH6s and the Company was ordered to cease production pending new supplies of wood and to burn all aircraft and components so far produced with low-grade timber. As a result of this directive, Grahame-White was forced to meet substantial wage bills for his idle workforce while he searched the country for suitable timber. The cost of these delays was to be the subject of a complex legal battle that would be waged between Grahame-White and the Government for many years to come.

In the meantime, those people who lived and worked around Hendon aerodrome were still forcefully reminded of the war by the occasional Gotha and Zeppelin raids in the vicinity. On the night of 19 October, Zeppelin L45, one of thirteen German airships that set out to bomb England that night, followed the Midland railway south from Northampton to drop a number of bombs in the area. Flying in the teeth of a gale which kept most of the defending aircraft grounded, L45 continued its southerly course taking it over central London where it dropped more bombs on Camberwell, Piccadilly and Hither Green, killing a total of twenty-one people. The airship was eventually forced down in southern France by a combination of appalling weather, engine failure and fatigue. The raid proved to be the last large scale Zeppelin attack on England of the war.

Nevertheless, pressure from the services for a seemingly never-ending supply of pilots steadily increased during the year and the average number of pupils under training at the Hendon schools at any one time during the second half of 1917 topped the one hundred mark. One of those, who took his first flight in a Grahame-White Boxkite on 21 November, was a young Canadian veteran of the Macedonian campaign who had recently transferred to the RFC, Lester Bowles Pearson. Two weeks later, Pearson was one of many to be presented to their Majesties King George V and Queen Mary during a visit to Hendon aerodrome on 4 December. The main purpose of the Royal visit, a relatively rare occurrence at the time, was to tour the Grahame-White Company factories, after which the King and Queen declared themselves pleased with what they had seen – and so they should have been.

In many ways the Company was a model employer, providing for its employees housing in the form of a self-contained estate named Aeroville built close to the aerodrome boundary off Colindale Avenue, and with welfare facilities and a modern staff canteen. The firm's annual sports day was attended by Grahame-White and his wife, and regular outings were arranged for employees and their families. By the standards of the day, working conditions were better than most, with spacious modern workshops and well-lit drawing offices which covered some fifty acres, accommodating a workforce of over 3,000 by

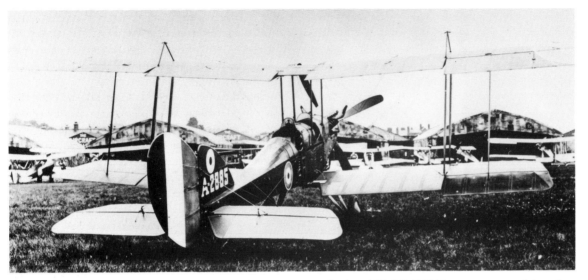

A BE2E in the No 2 Acceptance Park in 1917. Its canvas aeroplane storage sheds were erected in front of Hendon's original wooden sheds occupied by The Aircraft Manufacturing Company (AIRCO).

the end of 1917. At the time of the Royal visit, aircraft were leaving the factory at the rate of forty a week.

1918 saw little respite in the war effort and this was reflected by the activity at Hendon. Frederick Koolhoven's first design for BAT, the FK22 Bantam Mark I, a small single-seat fighter with a wooden monocoque fuselage, made its first flight on 19 January in the hands of company test pilot, Peter Legh. The following month, an improved version of the troublesome DH9 which had first appeared the previous October, the 400hp Liberty-engined DH9A, was flown by Capt 'Benny' Hucks and on 4 March the AIRCO DH10 twin-engined bomber made its maiden flight at Hendon.

On 27 March, His Majesty King George V sent a telegram of congratulations to Major-General J.M. Salmond, now GOC, RFC in the Field, and all ranks of the air services of the British Empire, on the air support afforded to the land forces in checking the German advance towards the Channel ports.

On 1 April, the Royal Air Force was created, merging the Royal Naval Air Service and the Royal Flying Corps into a separate Service of the Crown. This resulted from the Government's acceptance of a report on Air Organisation drawn up by General

Smuts, a strong supporter of General Hugh Montague Trenchard who had commanded the RFC since 1915, that had been presented to the War Cabinet on 17 August 1917. The recommendations of this report were strongly resisted by the Navy lobby led by Noel Pemberton-Billings MP, a staunch critic of Trenchard and his Director of Air Organisation, Major-General W. Sefton Brancker.

With the creation of the RAF, Hendon ceased to be a Royal Naval Air Station, but for some reason, did not become a Royal Air Force Station. Hendon was referred to by the authorities simply as No 2 Aircraft Acceptance Park. The unit occupied fourteen aeroplane storage sheds covering some forty acres of the aerodrome by early 1918, the function of which included the erection, testing, fitting of instruments, guns etc, and delivery by air, or storage of three main types of machines; the DH9 from AIRCO, Waring & Gillow and B.W. Berwick & Co; the DH9A from AIRCO, the Handley Page 0/400 from Handley Page Ltd, and the Sopwith Camel from Hooper Ltd at Wembley, and British Nieuport. The personnel employed on the site had more than doubled in a year to over 1,000 with the monthly average total output rising from 27 to 170 machines. Amongst the many pilots to make their way to Hendon at the end of a leave in 'Blighty' to collect new aircraft and ferry them back to units in France was Captain A.H. Curtis. He had made his first flight at Hendon on 13 July 1914 in a 50hp Beatty-Wright biplane with instructor Edouard Baumann and on 15 May 1918 returned to the aerodrome to collect a brand-new 200hp BHP-powered DH9 (C6175) to fly it across the Channel to Marquise (Boulogne) via Lympne.

With the rapid expansion of the Aircraft Park, the remaining civilian schools, with the exception of the Grahame-White School, had moved out during the early months of the year; Beatty and Ruffy-Baumann to Cricklewood and the London & Provincial to Acton, although all remained part of the RFC School of Instruction and, until 1 April, commanded by Major L.F. Richard.

Coinciding with the creation of the RAF was the arrival over the Western Front of the United States Air Service aircraft, but the new service was suffering heavy casualties during its first months of existence. Many of its most experienced combat pilots fell in a renewed German onslaught including a number who added to Hendon's roll-of honour. On 20 April, twenty-one-year-old Major Richard Raymond-Barker, MC, another graduate of the Ruffy-Baumann School, had the dubious distinction of becoming Manfred von Richthofen's last victim, after he himself had shot down seven enemy aircraft. Australian Captain R.A. Little, who trained at Hendon in October 1915, was credited with shooting down forty-seven enemy aircraft by the time he lost his life on the night of 27 May, ironically when attacking Gothas over London whilst on leave in England. Fellow Australian Major B.S. Dallas died three weeks later fighting three Fokker DrIs over Lievin having scored thirty-nine victories. Then on 26 July, Britain's most successful fighter pilot, Major Edward 'Mick' Mannock, crashed in flames over the Western Front. His unofficial score of combat victories stood at seventy-three at the time of his death, although it was widely accepted that he credited many more victories to fellow pilots. Nearly a year after his death, Mannock was awarded a posthumous Victoria Cross.

The day after Mannock's last flight, a new RAF unit was established at Hendon, a Home Communications Squadron equipped with four DH4s tasked with the transport of VIPs and urgent dispatches between England and France.

On 30 August, British troops crossed the Somme and by October German forces were in retreat on all fronts. Nevertheless, new combat aircraft continued to take to the air for the first time at Hendon during the dying months of the war, such as the promising British Nieuport Nighthawk. No less than 11,050 Nighthawks had been ordered in August from thirteen sub-contractors including the Grahame-White Aviation Co Ltd. Having completed his Avro 504 and DH6 contracts, ironically the latter

The AIRCO DH10 Mk II No C8659. The twin-engined bomber developed from the unsuccessful DH3, was first flown at Hendon by 'Benny' Hucks on 4 March 1917.

machine had been declared 'much too safe' for instructional purposes, and the type had become redundant even before the contract was completed, Grahame-White was again soliciting the newly-formed Air Ministry for further orders for his 3,000 workforce. At the beginning of 1918 he began publishing articles and placing advertisements extolling the virtues of his aerodrome and flying school for the aerial tourist and private flyer, and advocating the benefits of aerial transport to all parts of the British Empire and across the Atlantic. The company also designed a large twin-engined bomber, the G-W E9 Ganymedes. Powered by two Beardmore engines, the bomber was rolled out for its maiden flight in front of the assembled workforce to be christened with a bottle of champagne by Grahame-White's wife, Ethel. However, as the Ganymedes commenced its take-off run, the undercarriage collapsed and the aircraft was unceremoniously dragged back to the workshops for modifications.

By the end of October, the expansion of No 2 Aircraft Acceptance Park was officially complete and most of its output was being assigned to the newly-created Inter-Allied Independent Air Force, under the control of Major-General Sir Hugh Trenchard, to carry out concentrated attacks on German industry and commerce.

At 11 am on 11 November, an Armistice was signed with Germany and hostilities ceased. There can be no doubt that Hendon's contribution to the war effort had been considerable. Between August 1914 and November 1918, 490 military pilots received primary flying training at the aerodrome of which no less than six, out of a total of nineteen officers and other ranks of the flying services, were awarded the Victoria Cross for conspicuous gallantry in the air. Nearly 8,000 aircraft, out of a total British production total of some 55,000, were produced by the half a dozen factories surrounding the aerodrome; 5,500 by AIRCO, which by 1917/18 employed some 15,000 local people. However, with the end of hostilities, most of the factories and their employees faced an uncertain future as indeed did Hendon aerodrome, which on official Air Ministry documents was described as 'Not at present on the list of permanent stations.'

3 POLITICS AND PAGEANTS

THE PIONEERS BOW OUT

With the coming of peace, Britain's aviation industry, which had been created from virtually nothing in four years of war, was thrown into confusion. Massive War Office contracts were cancelled overnight with no compensation offered to those unfortunate manufacturers who had invested vast sums of money into gearing up for production. For Claude Grahame-White, the situation was even more devastating as his aerodrome was still in the hands of the War Office and there seemed little prospect of it being returned to its owner in the immediate future. Again, within days of the armistice, Grahame-White resorted to writing a long and impassioned letter to Winston Churchill. The letter, dated 22 November 1918, graphically illustrated the frustrations and confusion that followed at the end of the war, the full text of it read as follows;

Dear Mr Churchill

As managing director of one of the oldest pre-war pioneer aircraft firms, I come to you, as a court of last appeal, to lay before you certain facts; and with this knowledge in your possession, I am convinced you will not allow any harsh and unjust treatment by a Government department over which you preside to precipitate my firm, within ten days of the signing of the armistice, to utter ruin and annihilation.

It is I am sure within your knowledge that since August, 1914, I have with the financial assistance and approval of Ministry built up on the then existing foundations a huge aircraft factory and organisation, now employing close on 3,000 hands, and have entered into certain obligations to repay large Government loans over given periods, and have always been assured the support and special consideration of your department to enable me to carry out these obligations.

Some four months ago I notified the Supply Department that the metal shops of the factory were rapidly approaching a period when more work would be required in order to keep them employed; and we were then instructed to make immediate arrangements to construct forty Super-Handley Page biplanes. After turning the whole of my technical staff on to this job, and sending some designers to Beardmore in Scotland, and myself going to Harland and Wolff at Belfast to obtain all particulars in connection with the machines, these instructions were subsequently cancelled, and we were told to make immediate arrangements for the construction of 500 Sopwith Snipe Dragonfly machines. We again went very carefully into the construction of these machines, obtained blue prints, and started to lay out our shops to cope immediately with the work, as by this time several of our metal departments were in urgent need of work.

Just as we were embarking on this contract we were notified by the Supply Department that it had been decided to replace this contract by one for a similar number of Nieuport Nighthawk machines, and requesting us to cancel work on the Sopwith Snipe machines, and immediately to attend a conference at the Air Board to deal with this amended programme. We were subsequently instructed to proceed with the construction of 500 of these Nighthawk machines, and were sent blue prints, and were told to make 1,500 complete sets of metal fittings for these machines.

We had just got going on this job, for which the shop was waiting, when to our amazement we were instructed not to proceed with the Nighthawk machines, but that it had been decided to retain our firm on the construction of Avro machines (Avro 504), and that a contract was being prepared for us to construct a further 500 of these machines.

By this time it was difficult for me to realize that the Department was treating the matter seriously, and I somewhat naturally became alarmed at the constant and never-ending changes which had been made in the instructions conveyed to me over a period of three months, during the whole of which time the position in our metal shops was daily becoming more serious owing to the lack of work.

While awaiting the instructions to proceed with the 500 Avros I duly notified the Department that I had large numbers of hands standing idle, due to this constant change of programme; and then came the armistice. On Thursday, November 12th, the day following the signing of the armistice, I called at the Air Board and saw Col. Bartley, and requested immediate instructions how I was to proceed, in view of the fact that I had not received any confirmation of the order for 500 Avros, and that the whole of my metal-shop hands were now idle.

He requested that I should hold on for a day or two, as by the following Thursday he expected the whole policy and future programme of the Supply Department to be formulated.

I called daily without obtaining any definite instructions whatsoever, being merely put off indefinitely, and during the whole of this period I have had between 800 and 1,000 hands practically idle.

Yesterday I saw Lord Weir, who informed me that this was a matter over which he had no control, and referred me to Sir Arthur Duckham, whom I saw subsequently, and he promised to look into the matter, and asked me to return at 4.30pm. This I did, and at 7pm was informed that no work would be given to our metal shops, and that we were to discharge the whole of our hands in this department — a procedure which entails not only the paying of a week's wages in lieu of notice, but also the annihilation of the whole factory organisation.

You will I am sure appreciate that this situation has arisen, and is primarily due, not to the armistice but to the constant changes in programme, and indecision, of the Supply Department long before this date; and in any case I can hardly imagine that within ten days of the signing of the armistice it can be the policy of the Ministry to cripple and render impotent an important aircraft factory which has been brought into existence and fostered by the Ministry, and which I suggest should be accorded adequate support for a period at any rate in keeping with the provisions of the Contracts' Break Clause, in order to enable us to secure other work, and to tide us over a period during which we may formulate our future programme.

This suggested drastic action of discharging all our metal-shop hands will naturally have a far-reaching influence on the whole future of our important undertaking. It is indeed nothing short of driving us to ruin, and is bound to render it impossible for us to meet our obligations to repay the £200,000 loan still outstanding, more especially as the whole of remunerative aerodrome property is still in the hands of the Government, and we are therefore unable to formulate any post-war programme in this connection until we are informed when we shall regain possession of our property. We are still under Government control, and it was only yesterday that we were verbally told that we were at liberty to obtain any work outside the Government control in order to keep the factory running; and in the same breath we were instructed to discharge between 800 and 1,000 of our metal-workers.

Nor does this fully state my case. You may recollect that I was advanced £320,000 by the Ministry in March last; £120,000 of which was recoverable by deductions from contracts, the balance repayable by equal payments over a period of three years after the ratification of peace. The £120,000 has already been repaid, and I have faithfully kept all my obligations to date; but now at this difficult transition period from war to peace I am faced by financial difficulties by reason of the Ministry's dilatory and indifferent attitude in regard to claims I have lodged long since for sums amounting in the aggregate to over £300,000, in addition to sums due to us for goods delivered, amounting to a further £100,000; and these figures, substantial though they are, do not include any claim for the impressment of the aerodrome, which was taken under DORA and on which I have been paying all the outgoings ever since impressment.

From the foregoing you will I am sure realize that although the Government are my debtors to the tune of between £300,000 and £400,000, I am with no warning whatsoever, and with no chance of seeking work elsewhere, driven to disperse an organisation which it has taken four years to build up, and which, if the Ministry could have maintained it for two or three months, would have enabled me to fill the factory with other work and so render it possible to keep all hands fully employed, and incidentally to keep my financial obligation to the Ministry.

Owing to the delay in settling the before-mentioned claims I am bereft of all working capital — being unable thereby to pay my current trade creditors — and am being rushed to ruin and crippled by a procrastinating and unsympathetic Government department. I think I should bring it to your notice, here, in order to avoid misapprehension, that since the beginning of the war I have taken nothing out of my business in the form of dividends or other special remuneration, and I have received nothing beyond my salary as provided for in the Ministry of Munitions agreement.

I do now with every confidence appeal to you as the Chief of this great and important department to have my case sympathetically treated on its merits and to be assisted with consideration through this admittedly difficult transition period. Time is, in this connection, the crux of the whole problem. Any delay will inevitably wreck this important and, if I may say so, national enterprise. While apologising for the length, I do feel that I should inform you that a rumour of these impending discharges is circulating in the factory. A very ugly attitude is in consequence developing, and it may be necessary for us to request police protection; and unless our financial position is assured by the immediate payment of substantial sums on account of our claims we shall be forced to dismiss the whole of the wood-workers and aggrevate the situation. If you could grant me an interview I could furnish you with any further details you require. In conclusion, may I crave your prompt consideration for this very urgent matter.

Yours very truly,

Claude Grahame-White

This uncompromising letter was of great importance from many points of view. It not only vividly illustrated the precarious position in which many manufacturers involved in the munitions industry found themselves at the end of hostilities, but it clearly pointed to the subjects of future conflict between Grahame-White and the Government — principally the amounts of money claimed to be owed to each other and the future of the aerodrome — and highlighted the lack of trust that already existed between the two parties involved.

Of more immediate concern, however, was how to keep his now considerably reduced workforce gainfully occupied. Nonetheless, when a large number of the company employees were inevitably made redundant there was no rioting. Most factories in the area were in the same position and all were required to lay off at least some, if not all their workforce. The British Nieuport and General Aircraft Company had contracts for no less than 1,100 Nighthawks cancelled after the armistice and the company practically ceased to exist following a merger with the British Aerial Transport Co Ltd. In desperation, Grahame-White returned to the motor trade in order to keep the factories working. Hands from the metal-shops were put to work reconditioning surplus army lorries, Leylands, Albions etc, as well as Rolls-Royce armoured cars — the latter were fitted with new limousine body shells to become once again, the epitomy of the luxury car. The products from the factories were sold at weekly motor auctions held in one of the Grahame-White company hangars at Hendon. A small two-seat cyclecar powered by a 3½ hp Precian air-cooled engine, called the Grahame-White Duckboard, also went into production, in competition with the Blériot Whippet being manufactured at Brooklands, with more than 100 per week leaving Hendon by the end of 1919. A depleted force of wood-workers, meanwhile, were utilising the vast stocks of seasoned wood held by the company to produce a range of household furniture.

There was still little sign of the aerodrome being de-requisitioned and released to its founder, although Hendon could hardly be termed as a vital operational airfield. An Air Ministry record of the time described Hendon thus; 'Soil, heavy clay. Surface, moderate, inclined to become wet. Surface drainage is being carried out. Fairly level. General surroundings, somewhat enclosed. Railway with high embankment bounds the Aerodrome on the east; the surrounding district is populous. The fields are of moderate size and there are many trees. The country rises to the east.'

No 2 Acceptance Park was in the process of being wound down with hundreds of aircraft in various stages of erection being placed in open storage on the aerodrome. The only active unit at Hendon was the Communications Squadron which became the No 1 (Communications) Squadron, part of 86 (Communications) Wing which formed at Hendon

Three Handley Page 0/400 bombers were adapted to carry six VIP passengers and operated by No 1 (Comms) Squadron. D8326, built by the British Caudron Co in 1918 was named His Majesty's Air Liner (HMAL) *Silver Star*.

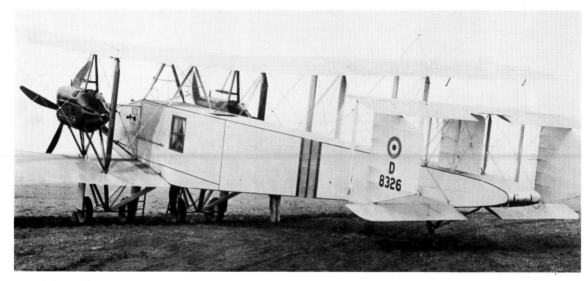

on 13 December 1918. Equipped with eight DH4s, eight Handley Page 0/400s and two Martinsyde F4 Buzzards, the squadron provided high speed transport for VIPs and urgent dispatches between London and the Peace Conference at Versailles. AIRCO had modified a number of DH4s to carry two passengers, in addition to the pilot, who were seated facing each other in the rear fuselage, with access through a hinged section in the cabin roof. Known as the DH4A, one of these aircraft was issued to the Communications squadron at Hendon, named HMAL (His Majesty's Air Liner) *Lady Iris*. Two of the 0/400s, HMALs *Silver Star* and *Great*

Britain, were adapted to carry six and eight VIP passengers respectively, in a well-appointed cabin fitted with tables and reading lights. On 10 January, the squadron began regular passenger and mail flights to Buc (Paris) thus creating history by carrying the first post-war civilian passengers across the Channel.

As a result of the first post-war General Election held in December 1918, the Coalition Government, headed by Lloyd George, was returned to power and wasted no time in dismantling the country's vast war machine. In January 1919, the Prime Minister announced that the days of the fledgling Royal Air

The first production AIRCO
DH4A seen over Hendon in 1919.
This aircraft began regular
passenger and mail services with
No 1 (Communications)
Squadron between Hendon and
Buc near Paris.

Force as a separate department were numbered. This move was immediately opposed by Churchill, Lloyd George's Secretary of State for War and Air, who threw his weight behind Trenchard's vigorous campaign to retain the RAF's independence. In the meantime, Britain's so-recently thriving aviation industry was in limbo. It was clear that even if the RAF should win its fight for survival, it would not be in a position to place any substantial orders for new equipment in the foreseeable future. At the same time, the ban imposed on civil flying in 1914 was still in force, owing to the fact that the Country remained technically at a State of War until Germany signed a Peace Treaty. There was, therefore, no immediate prospect of a market for new commercial designs.

In the meantime the pace of life at Hendon in the early months of 1919 had reduced considerably, with one of the few events of interest being the presentation of three newly-built Sopwith Snipes, one a gift from the City of Leicester, to the Canadian Government on 21 January. The aircraft were to be unsuccessful entries in the Toronto to New York air race held later in the year.

Pilots of No 1 (Comms) Squadron battled through the winter weather to carry Government delegates and mail to France in an effort to hasten the Peace process at Versailles. As an example of their determination to complete the task, Capt Knott, flying one of the Squadron's DH4s on 19 March with a special despatch destined for the Prime Minister, was forced down by bad weather at Marquise (Boulogne) and completed his journey by catching a train to Paris. During this period one of the Buzzards set a record by flying the 245 miles London to Paris route in 1hr 15min. At the end of March, the Squadron moved to Kenley, having flown 117 passengers and more than 100 bags of mail in 136 sorties from Hendon.

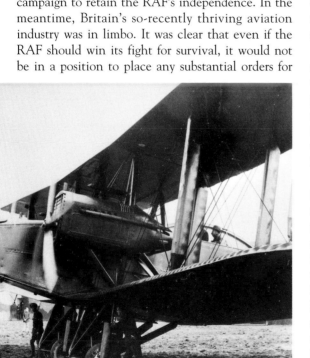

A Handley Page 0/400 about to take-off from Hendon in January 1919 on a demonstration flight for Indian journalists. Note the camouflaged hangar in the background.

As far as the RAF was concerned Hendon was now nothing more than a parking place for several hundred brand new but unwanted aeroplanes. However, in an effort to ward off total closure, the few remaining manufacturers in the vicinity continued to roll out prototypes of passenger-carrying aeroplanes in the hope that civil flying restrictions would soon end and the Government would support a network of British international airlines. The first to appear was the Airco DH16, a four-seat adaptation of the DH9, which made its first flight in March destined for Holt Thomas' Aircraft Transport & Travel Ltd (AT&T). An AT&T DH4 had already made an unscheduled

'civil' flight on 1 March when it was chartered by Sir Woodman Burbidge, the chairman of Harrods, for a flight to Brussels. A month later, Frederick Koolhoven's BAT FK26, Britain's first purely civil transport aircraft seating four passengers, made its maiden flight at Hendon with Peter Legh at the controls. Less than a month later, Legh was to lose his life when the prototype BAT FK25 Basilisk crashed on test flight from Hendon on 3 May. The high performance single-seat fighter caught fire in the air and crashed at East Finchley.

In the meantime, the authorities had lifted the ban on civil flying over the Easter weekend, 17-22 April, when a number of new aircraft were seen by

The AIRCO DH16, a four-seat adaptation of the DH9, made its first flight from Hendon in March 1919. It became one of the first British airliners serving with George Holt Thomas' Aircraft Transport & Travel Ltd (AT&T).

This British Aerial Transport Co Ltd (BAT) FK23 Bantam, F1657 later K-155, was flown to victory in a ten-lap race by Cyril Turner at the first post-war meeting — at Hendon — the Whitsun one on 7 June 1919.

commercial flight took place on the same day when an AT&T DH9, G-EAAA, left Hendon carrying a consignment of newspapers bound for Bournemouth, only to crash in fog at Portsmouth.

Meanwhile, on the other side of the Atlantic four giant US Navy flying-boats were making preparations for a trans-Atlantic flight via Newfoundland, the Azores and Lisbon. Four weeks later the surviving flying-boat, a Curtiss NC-4, was escorted into Plymouth harbour by three Felixstowe F2As of the Royal Air Force, at the end of a 3,925 mile flight completed in 57hr 16min flying time. Lieutenant-Commander A.C. Read, captain of the NC-4, and his five-man crew were invited to Hendon where a reception was held in their honour. Major Christopher Draper, Cyril Turner and Handley Page's American test pilot, Clifford Podger, demonstrated several BAT FK23 Bantams in civil markings, while Harry Hawker flew the two-seat Sopwith Gnu. Grahame-White auctioned a flight with Hawker in the Gnu, with a Miss Daisy King paying the princely sum of sixty guineas for the privilege. After a week of celebrations in London, the NC-4 crew were flown to Joyce Green (Dartford) to begin their journey home in a BAT FK26 escorted by Cyril Turner in a Bantam.

the public for the first time at an impromptu air show at Hendon. Amongst them was the Grahame-White GW E6 Bantam, a small single-seat sporting biplane, designed by the Frenchman E. Boudot, who was responsible for the Nestler Scout which was involved in a fatal crash at Hendon two years earlier. An AT&T DH9 and DH16 gave joyrides as did an Airco-owned DH6 which became the first British aeroplane to carry civil markings when it was allocated the registration K-100.

All restrictions on civil flying were finally lifted on 1 May following the publication of the Air Navigation Regulations. The first official post-war

The first post-war aerial meeting took place at Hendon during the Whitsun weekend. On Saturday 7 June, Lt G.R. Hicks won a cross-country handicap flying an Avro 504K and the following day Cyril

Turner won 100 guineas and the Anglo-American Oil Co Cup flying the BAT Bantam K-155 to victory in a ten-lap race. Two weeks later, France's third highest scoring First World War ace, Charles Nungesser, was invited to test fly a BAT Bantam, registered K-123, at Hendon during a visit to Britain.

Although Hendon remained firmly in the Government's grip, Grahame-White, determined to marshall public support behind his campaign to regain control of his aerodrome, managed to organise the fourth Aerial Derby in an effort to re-establish the 'Hendon Habit'. The 'Victory' Aerial Derby held on 21 June attracted sixteen entries for the event run over two laps of a round London course, a total distance of 189 miles. Capt Gerald Gathergood led the field home in an Airco DH4R produced especially for the event in less than fifteen days. The clipped-wing DH4R, K-141, powered by a Napier Lion engine, won at an average speed of 129.3 mph thus setting a new British closed circuit record. A Falcon-engined Martinsyde F4, K-152, flown by R.H. Nisbet finished in second place at an average speed of 124.61 mph while Major C. Draper took fourth place in the BAT Bantam. Major R.M. Carr entered the Grahame-White Bantam but failed to finish the course. Two weeks later it was written-off during a cross-country race with Grahame-

The Grahame-White E6 Bantam, a sporting biplane designed by the Frenchman E. Boudot and flown by Major R.M. Carr, failed to finish the course and was written off two weeks later.

The British Nieuport Company's promising fighter, the Nighthawk, which was cancelled at the end of the war, was entered in the Victory Aerial Derby on 21 June 1919.

White's chief pilot, H. Chamberlayne, at the controls. As a side-show to the Derby, Capt Frank T. Courtney looped the twin-engined Boulton & Paul Bourges 1A designed by Grahame-White's ex-designer, J.D. North.

It must have seemed to many that the good days were returning to Hendon during the summer months of 1919. Germany had eventually been forced to sign a Peace Treaty at Versailles on 28 June and on 1 July Claude Grahame-White opened his most ambitious post-war venture — the London Flying Club. Situated on the southern side of Airport Road where a separate airfield had been created, the Club featured a lavish sixty-room clubhouse, no less than thirty hard tennis courts, two polo grounds and an eighteen-hole golf course.

The Flying Club itself was equipped with six Avro 504s for training and pleasure flying while three Government surplus Blackburn Kangaroos, originally designed as long-range bombers but

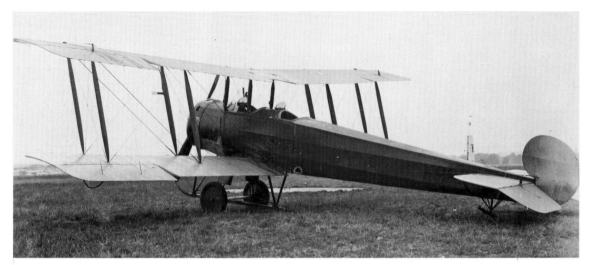

One of six Avro 504Ks operated by the London Flying Club.

modified to carry seven passengers, were available for joyflights and parachute jumping. On 13 July, an AT&T DH9, G-EAAC, flown by Capt H.G. 'Jerry' Shaw, an ex No 1 (Comms) Squadron pilot, flew the first international charter flight between Hendon and Paris, Le Bourget.

Regular air shows and races again brought the crowds to Hendon although the international flavour of the meetings which proved so popular before the war was the missing ingredient. Typical of the 1919 events was the Hendon Trophy Race flown over a twenty-mile course around Bittacy Hill on 26 July and won by Major Draper in the BAT FK24 Baboon, G-EACO.

The Air Ministry's argument for retaining control of Hendon Aerodrome appeared to have less and less validity as the year progressed. No 2 Aircraft Acceptance Park had been redesignated No 1 Aircraft Salvage Depot by mid-1919, little more than a dump for hundreds of surplus RAF aircraft, serviceable engines — offered at 25/- each (£1.25) — and thousands of spare parts. Here, factory-fresh front-line aircraft could be bought by anyone with a valid pilot's certificate for a few pounds enabling them to become instant fighter aces.

Twenty-year-old Philip Townsend and a colleague, both veterans of the Western Front flying DH4 Army Co-operation two-seaters, saw notice of a sale of Government aircraft at Hendon whilst awaiting their demob at Uxbridge. The pair travelled by bus to the airfield where they each bought an SE5A for £5, had them filled up, tested, and flew them for a memorable thirty minutes. However, with little immediate prospect of a job and being unable to afford £10 for a Certificate of Airworthiness, they had to sell the SE5s back to the depot for £4.10/- (£4.50) and reluctantly walk away from Hendon.

The Disposals Board's policy of selling almost new aeroplanes at give-away prices highlighted the problems of aircraft manufacturers striving to sell new commercial types costing hundreds, or even thousands of pounds each. In August 1919, the Grahame-White GW E7 'Aero Limousine' made its debut. This biplane, powered by two 320hp Rolls-Royce Eagle engines and seating five passengers in a comfortable enclosed cabin was capable of cruising at 104mph. The E7 attracted a great deal of interest but no sales. Airlines continued to rely on converted military types such as the DH4A, one of which was flown by Capt Gathergood carrying two passengers from Hendon to Edinburgh in a record 3hr 15min on 5 August.

The first scheduled daily international commercial flight anywhere in the world was flown on 25 August from London to Paris when a Hendon-based

This civilianised DH10 Amiens bomber was used by AT&T to fly scheduled mail flights for the Post Office between Hendon and Renfrew, Scotland during the national rail strike in October 1919.

G-EAJO

AT&T DH16 flown by Capt Cyril Patteson took off from Hounslow, a customs airport, with four passengers and landed at Le Bourget 2hr 30min later. Two months later the fortunes of Britain's underfinanced fledgling airlines, less than £1 million having been made available by the Government for the support of civil aviation in Britain at the end of the war, received a double boost from a national rail strike and the announcement of an official civil air-mail service by the Post Office and the Air Ministry. From 7 October, British Aerial Transport's embryonic airline, managed by Major Jack Savage, operated scheduled flights from Hendon to Birmingham, Manchester and Newcastle using the company's FK 26s while AT&T, which had recently appointed Major-General Sir Sefton Brancker as its Managing Director, flew a civil DH10, G-EAJO, between Hendon and Renfrew. At the same time Grahame-White's Kangaroo flew mail to Newcastle via Hounslow. However, following the settlement of the rail strike, demand for scheduled internal commercial flights fell to nil.

On 22 October it was announced that J.C. Porte, a leading figure in the development of the Hendon Aerodrome both before and during the war, had died from a combination of poor health and overwork at the early age of thirty-five years.

By the end of the year No 1 Aircraft Salvage Depot was closed after Handley Page Ltd bought up the Disposals Board's entire surplus stock, which was valued at £100,000,000, for a fraction of its worth. All the airframes, engines and parts were subsequently moved to Croydon to be marketed by the Aircraft Disposal Co Ltd, known as Airdisco, a Handley Page subsidiary.

In Parliament, the fight to ensure the RAF's survival continued unabated and in December Air Marshal Sir Hugh Trenchard, Chief of the Air Staff, submitted a scheme for the permanent organization of the Air Force which was presented to both Houses by Winston Churchill. Although the scheme, which made provision for six home squadrons plus two training wings with nineteen overseas squadrons, was accepted in principle as was the RAF's independence, the annual cost of the RAF was to be limited to £15 million with personnel cut down to 29,730 officers and men. The Air Force had thus been reduced to less than one-tenth of its wartime strength. It is interesting to note that Trenchard's Memorandum made no mention of Hendon although Cranwell, Halton, Manston and Uxbridge were listed for future development.

Nevertheless, memories of the pre-war record-breaking flights were revived when F.S. Cotton set off from Hendon on 2 February in a DH14A, G-EAPY, a civil version of the Airco DH14 Okapi, an unsuccessful two-seat day bomber, at the start of an attempt on the London to Cape Town record. The attempt was abandoned following a forced

The AIRCO DH14A left Hendon on 2 February 1920 at the start of an attempt on the London to Cape Town record. Two days later the attempt was abandoned after a forced landing in Italy.

Making its first flight from Hendon in 1920 was the AIRCO DH9R, a streamlined racing version of the DH9 day bomber.

landing in Italy which coincided with the departure of two RAF flyers who left Brooklands bound for South Africa; they arrived in Cape Town on 20 March. Yet more types aimed at the as yet almost non-existent civil market continued to be constructed and make their maiden flights at Hendon during the year. The first of these was the prototype of AIRCO's first airliner, the DH18, a large eight-seat biplane powered by a single 450hp Napier Lion and this made its first flight in February. It subsequently entered service with AT&T in April on the Croydon to Paris route only to be written-off a few months later.

A few weeks prior to the DH18's flight, Major Draper had flown the BAT FK27 Racer for the first time. On 23 March, Draper, who had finished the war with a score of twelve enemy aeroplanes, was seriously injured at Hendon in a BAT Bantam which spun into the ground from a height of 3,500ft. He was lucky to be dragged from the wreckage by Grahame-White's pilots, Chamberlayne and Courtney, who witnessed the accident.

However, all was not bad news as the Aerodrome was about to regain some of its enormous pre-war popularity. The fifth Aerial Derby took place on 24 July and was flown over the same course as the previous year. F.T. Courtney won the event at an average speed of 153.45mph followed home by Bert Hinkler in an Avro 534 Baby, G-EACQ. One of a

The Grahame-White Co Ltd Hucks starter, invented by Benny Hucks, AIRCO's chief pilot for swinging propellers mechanically.

number of Britain's leading fighter pilots, Capt W.L. Jordan, credited with the destruction of thirty-one enemy aircraft during the war, finished in fifth place in one of three civilianised Sopwith Snipes, G-EAUW. Another Avro Baby, G-EAUG, flown by H.A. Hammersley, who downed eleven enemy aircraft, won the £100 Handicap prize at an average speed of 70.3mph.

Other entries of note included Harry Hawker flying Sopwith Rainbow No 13, G-EAKI, who was

The Fifth Aerial Derby was held at Hendon on 24 July 1920 and won by Frank Courtney in this Sopwith Semi-Quaver which he managed to overturn on landing after the race. He was only slightly injured.

be used for the staging of a huge air display. The first Royal Air Force Tournament was held on Saturday 30 July and featured nearly every type of aircraft then in service, with participation of most of the home-based units. The event was organised by a committee under the Chairmanship of Air Vice-Marshal Sir John Salmond and made up of serving officers, who included Flt Lt W.H. Longton. The committee asked for and received Claude Grahame-White's generous permission to use 'his' aerodrome. Moreover it was assisted by his manager, Mr Law, and pre-war press agent, Bernard Isaacs.

The programme of twelve events included formation flying by Snipes and Bristol Fighters; a mock 'dogfight' between a Martinsyde F4 and a captured Fokker DVII; stunt flying by an SE5A; a relay race with each team flying an Avro 504K, a Bristol Fighter and a Sopwith Snipe; and crazy flying by a BE2 and an Avro 504K. A trio of Handley Page V/1500 heavy bombers also flew in formation over the airfield and Grahame-White and AT&T aeroplanes gave joyrides before and after the main programme. Other non-military events included a parachute jump by twenty-one-year-old Miss Sylvia Boyden, and an exhibition flight by Harry Hawker in the Sopwith Swallow. The climax of the Tournament was the destruction by an HP 0/400 escorted by Sopwith Snipes of a 'set piece' model fort that had been constructed by RAF tradesmen using wings and unserviceable parts of aeroplanes.

disqualified for missing a turning point; Flight Lieutenant W.H. Longton DFC, another wartime ace with a score of seven to his credit, in a civilianised Sopwith Snipe, G-EAUV, and F.S. Cotton in the unsuccessful London–Cape Town DH14A which had been returned to Hendon for repair. Both of the latter fliers were forced to abandon the race following forced landings. Only one week after the Derby, enormous crowds, reminiscent of those that attended the pre-war meetings, flocked to Hendon to attend the biggest aeronautical event of the year.

Earlier in the year the Royal Air Force had finally announced its plans for Hendon; ironically it was to

Participating pilots in that first RAF Tournament included Flt Lts K. Park, J.M. Robb and J. Slessor who, although veterans of the war who had brought down more than thirty German aircraft between them, were only just beginning long and illustrious careers with the RAF. More than 60,000 spectators, including HRH Prince Henry, Winston Churchill and Sir Hugh Trenchard, attended the display which raised a total of £7,261.19s.2d for the newly created RAF Memorial Fund. The event was considered an outstanding success by all involved. The RAF thought it an ideal and inexpensive way of gaining public support for its continuing existence and announced that henceforward the Tournament would become an annual event. Grahame-White was able to make full use of his London Flying Club facilities during the busy summer months of 1920. His luxurious hotel was booked to capacity and Hendon was again firmly on the social scene.

However, the excitement generated by the Aerial Derby and RAF Tournament was only a respite from the hard commercial facts that beset civil aviation in the immediate post-war period. The autumn of

The entrance to the London Aerodrome, Hendon, in 1920.

1920 was to see the entire closure of what remained of Hendon's once thriving aero industry. In August, the British Aerial Transport Company ceased trading; this was followed a few weeks later, by AIRCO, which was forced to sell its assets to BSA (Birmingham Small Arms), a company which only wanted its buildings and had no interest in aviation. Holt Thomas, who had formed AIRCO in 1912, was however, able to give some financial support to Geoffrey de Havilland, his brilliant designer since 1914, to enable him to create his own company based at a small airfield at Stag Lane situated within a mile of the Edgware Road. But things were to get worse for Holt Thomas: his other company, and Britain's first airline, Aircraft Transport and Travel was forced to close down having made its last commercial flight on 15 December. The company assets were taken over by the Daimler Airline. By the end of the year Grahame-White had ceased to construct any more aircraft, his 'Aero Limousine' had been destroyed by fire in September, and he was managing to keep a small workforce occupied producing cyclecars, furniture and reconditioning surplus military vehicles to be sold at the Hendon auctions. His determination to regain control of the main aerodrome remained undiminished despite gloomy economic predictions and little sign of the Government relenting.

In February, Winston Churchill relinquished his dual appointment as Secretary of State for War and Air when he was succeeded by Capt the Hon F.E. Guest, who would be closely connected with Hendon in the years to come. The only aerial activity at Hendon during the first half of 1921 was restricted to that of the London Flying Club's Avro 504s and one remaining Kangaroo, as well as a few visiting aircraft. Unfortunately, yet another famous personality closely connected with Hendon since its pre-war heydays, was to be lost during this period. Harry Hawker, one of aviation's most experienced pilots, took off from Hendon on 21 July for a pre-Derby test flight in the Nieuport Goshawk and was killed outright when the aircraft caught fire in flight and crashed in a field at Burnt Oak, only a mile west of the airfield.

As a prelude to the Aerial Derby, Oxford and Cambridge University flying clubs held an aerial equivalent to the Boat Race at Hendon. Six surplus SE5As were purchased for the event from the Aircraft Disposal Company's depot at Croydon, with the race being for a £400 prize flown over three laps of a portion of the Derby course which included turning points at Epping and Hertford, a total distance of 129 miles. The Cambridge team won the event with ease, thanks to their opponents retiring, but although there was a deal of public interest in the event, it was never repeated. A rather subdued sixth Aerial Derby took place three days after Hawker's fatal crash and was won by J.H. James in the Nieuport Mars 1, a racing development of the

The aeroplanes gathered at Hendon for the 1921 RAF Tournament include an HP 0/400, Bristol Fighters, Avro 504s, a Sopwith Snipe, a Sopwith Dolphin, a BAT Bantam and an SE5A.

Nighthawk, which completed the course at a record speed of 163.8mph. Most of the entries comprised high-powered RAF surplus fighters, such as Flt Lt Longton in an SE5A, G-EAXS, Leslie Foot's Martinsyde F4, G-EAXB, H.S. Broad's slightly civilianised Sopwith Camel, G-EAWN, which was classified sixth, and C.F. Uwin's fourth-placed Bristol Bullet. Another old Hendon hand, Sqd Ldr A.H. Curtis, entered a BE2E, G-EAVS, in the Handicap section but was forced to withdraw at the last minute.

The second Royal Air Force Pageant, as it was now to be called, was held on Saturday 2 July and was attended by Their Majesties King George V and Queen Mary, and Queen Alexandra making a return visit to Hendon. They were accompanied by the Duke of York, the first member of the Royal Family to gain his Wings and recently promoted to Group Captain in the RAF. The sixteen events in the flying display followed the same successful mix as the previous year. Most of the participating aircraft were of wartime vintage, with the exception of the prototype Armstrong Whitworth Siskin and Westland Wagtail.

Major C. Draper returned to Hendon to lead a formation team, the RAF's first, of five Sopwith Snipes from the Central Flying School. Solo aerobatics were performed by Flg Off G. Bulman in a BAT FK23 Bantam fighter, F1653, Flt Lt Longton in a Camel, and Flt Lt J. Noakes who repeated his popular crazy flying routine in a red Avro 504K, J8332. Inter-station and HQ relay races were keenly contested; Snipes attacked Handley Page V/1500 bombers and shot down a Kite Balloon while Bristol Fighters, led by Group Captain H. Dowding, destroyed the Scappa Plain Enemy Village set-piece. During the afternoon the airship R33 flew over the aerodrome and Mr William Newell made another parachute descent over Hendon, this time from Grahame-White's Kangaroo. At the end of the day, the satisfied crowds made their slow journey home from Hendon eagerly looking forward to the next RAF Pageant.

Having acted as race promoter for the Oxford and Cambridge Air Race earlier in the year, Major J.C. Savage — an ex-Grahame-White mechanic and one time manager of Benny Hucks and the British Aerial Transport Company's airline — returned to Hendon in August to establish the Savage Skywriting Company. With a fleet of Airdisco SE5As, equipped with his patented smoke system, and with Cyril Turner, an ex-RFC ferry pilot and

BAT test pilot, as Chief Pilot, Savage was soon in demand by nationally-known companies who saw the advantages of having the name of their company written in fifty-feet high smoke letters in the sky over large cities. Savage ran the operation in some style from a suite at the London Flying Club and in May 1922, after months of experimentation using black smoke, one of his SE5s gave the first public demonstration of skywriting in Britain, using the more visible white smoke, over Hendon.

In June Major-General Sir W. Sefton Brancker was appointed as the Director of Civil Aviation in the department of the Under-Secretary of State for Air. By this time, few of Britain's unsubsidised airlines that were formed at the end of the war would be able to survive much longer against foreign competitors, most of which, particularly the French, were heavily subsidised by their respective governments. However, there were high hopes that Brancker would be able to achieve something positive for the country's civil aviation industry.

The impasse that Grahame-White and the Government had reached over the ownership of the Hendon Aerodrome was brought to a head coinciding with the announcement of Brancker's appointment. While holidaying with friends in the United States, Grahame-White was forced to cut short his visit when he received disturbing news that the Treasury was threatening to seize his factory and its assets in lieu of unpaid tax debts and

War Ministry loans granted during the war against future orders, and to appoint a receiver for the Company. Realising that this was a clumsy attempt to obtain the site cheaply, he hastily returned to England and with the support of his old ally, the *Daily Mail*, stepped up his campaign to discredit the government's actions. Although the threat of seizure was temporarily lifted, the dispute continued unabated.

In the meantime, 'Jimmy' James flying the Mars, also known as the Gloster Bamel, led the field home in the seventh Aerial Derby for the second year in succession at a speed of 177.8mph, well ahead of the second place Bristol Bullet, G-EATS, flown by Flt Lt Rollo de Haga Haig who finished with a speed of 145mph.

Despite wet weather, a record number of spectators attended the third RAF Aerial Pageant on 30 June to enjoy the now traditional programme of races, demonstrations, and stunt flying by Flt Lts Longton and Noakes. Another crowd pleaser was the dogfight, which this year was between three wartime 'aces', Sqd Ldr Roderick Hill, in a Liberty-engined DH10, fending off two SE5As flown by Flg Offs Bulman and Grinnel-Milne, considered by many the best yet seen at Hendon. New types shown for the first time in public included the Westland Weasel and the Avro Aldershot. Aircraft of the Fleet Air Arm made their first appearance at Hendon in the form of Blackburn Darts and the set-piece 'Desert Stronghold' was comprehensively destroyed by nine Bristol Fighters. At the end of the day the RAF Memorial Fund was better off by more than £3,000.

While the RAF Fund flourished, the Grahame-White Co Ltd balance sheet for 1922 showed another heavy loss and in view of the trade depression and the continuing uncertainty surrounding the ownership of the Aerodrome, Claude Grahame-White decided to replace his 'more or less unprofitable manufacturing business by a potentially profitable letting proposition'. Consequently all of his remaining workforce were paid off, with only a small staff being retained to ensure the upkeep of company property; a large proportion of the assets and stock-in-trade were subsequently sold by auction in order to secure the buildings for rental. In September Grahame-White wrote to Sir Sefton Brancker suggesting that the Civil Aviation Department should take over the Aerodrome and three of the buildings to establish it as the chief London Air Port, 'in view of the fact that Croydon has since been found to be unsuitable'. The price quoted for the rental of these rights was £10,000 per year: the offer was not taken up, hardly surprising in view of the Treasury's interest in the property! Croydon was eventually chosen to be developed as London's first international airport.

There was then the possibility of the London Hospitals group taking over the entire property for £25,000, a figure later raised to £75,000. But although this sum would have enabled Grahame-White to pay off his trade creditors and personal income tax, he was loath to sell it outright so long as the existing Government charges on the property remained. However, in November, the London Electric Railway Company announced its intention to extend the Golders Green Tube line through the Company's and his own personal property for which they were to pay an estimated £10,000. But the year ended with no solution to the problem of the Aerodrome's ownership in sight.

In the spring of 1923 a sale was held at Hendon of a number of aircraft owned by C.P.B. Ogilvie, a well-known dealer of the period. He had purchased most of the British Aerial Transport's aircraft when the company ceased trading, including the FK23 Bantam K-123 and two FK26s, G-EANI and G-EAFM, and a rare Austin Whippet G-EAPF, all of which were stored on the Aerodrome. The latter was sold to the well-known racing pilot, Flg Off F.O. 'Mongoose' Soden.

The 1923 RAF Pageant was noteworthy for many reasons. Apart from familiar flying events by RAF and Fleet Air Arm units including a mock dogfight between a Boulton & Paul Bourges and two Nighthawks, and a formation aerobatic display by five SE5As, the Pageant boasted the largest collection of new and experimental types yet seen.

These ranged from the 3hp ABC-powered Wren to the Aldershot plus the Westland Walrus, the Flycatcher, the Plover and the Grebe, another development of Folland's high performance successor to his SE5, the Nighthawk. Moreover, the Pageant was honoured with the presence of the King and Queen and the Duke of York, while the occasion was chosen for the new Duchess of York's first public engagement. The set-piece finale was another action packed Desert Battle, all of which helped to raise a total of £5,247 for the RAF Fund.

Following the growing success of the Aerial Pageants, Trenchard was anxious to preserve Hendon as an aerodrome in face of the threat of encroaching London suburbia — a threat that was considerably increased by the proposed extension of the tube line from Hampstead to Edgware. However, the Air Ministry did not have funds available to make a firm offer for the aerodrome that had any chance of being accepted, so the stalemate persisted for another year.

The Aerial Derby, which Grahame-White inaugurated in 1912, was finally abandoned in 1923 when Hendon was chosen for the start of the second King's Cup Air Race. The race was a handicap under the rules of the Royal Aero Club, organised by a committee chaired by Sir Sefton Brancker, and the Cup, which was presented by King George V, was awarded to the entrant of the aeroplane which first completed a circuit of Great Britain of approximately 850 miles. Amongst the entries who lined up for the start at Hendon on 13 July was Alan Cobham in George Robey's DH Moth; Henri Biard, winner of the 1922 Schneider Trophy, in a Supermarine Sea Eagle; Fred Raynham, a famous name in pre-war air racing in a Martinsyde; and Cyril Turner in one of Savage's SE5As. The Aerial Derby, run over 309 miles, was won by F.T. Courtney in a Siskin II, G-EBEU, entered by J.D. Siddeley, at a speed of 149 mph. Larry Carter, flying a Gloster Grebe G-EBHA, won a £100 prize for the fastest circuit but was forced to withdraw on the second circuit.

In another attempt to stimulate private flying the Secretary of State for Air offered a £500 prize to encourage the building of an economic light aeroplane suitable for club and private flying. A series of Light Aeroplane trials was held at Lympne and was followed by the Royal Aero Club's Lightplane Demonstrations at Hendon on 23 October. Amongst those taking part were Bert Hinkler in an Avro 560 and H.A. Hammersley in a similar Avro 558, neither of which won a prize and the competition failed in its aim with only one of the competitors attaining quantity production.

In January 1924, Claude Grahame-White wrote to the Government with a proposal to lease the aerodrome to the Air Ministry for a period of twenty years in yet another effort to resolve the protracted deadlock. However, the Air Council replied that it was essential that the London Aerodrome should be acquired immediately for the Home Defence Scheme. Accordingly the £3 million increase in the Air estimates introduced by the Secretary of State for Air in the House of Commons on 11 March allowed not only for the formation of eight new squadrons for Home Defence during 1924-25, but provision for the outright purchase of the London Aerodrome.

While the complex procedure of offer and counter-offer was being initiated by the Government's and Grahame-White's solicitors, the RAF mounted their most ambitious Pageant to date. The Duke and Duchess of York were again present on 28 June, as was the King of Denmark, to witness not only the now familiar demonstrations by Snipes, DH9As and Avro 504Ks, but a polished display of formation flying by five Nieuport-Delage Type 29C.1 fighters of the French Deuxième Régiment de Chasse, the first foreign unit to be invited to the Pageant. New types shown were the Handley Page Hyderabad, Vickers Virginia, Hawker Woodcock, Avro Andover Ambulance and another unsuccessful contender in the previous year's Light Aeroplane trials, the DH53 Humming Bird. The grand finale of the 1924 Pageant was a set piece attack on two 'enemy' ships by Flycatchers, Darts and a Seagull amphibian of the newly-separate Fleet Air Arm.

Soon after the RAF had vacated Hendon for another year, the Colindale Tube station, situated a few hundred yards from the aerodrome entrance, opened on 18 August. Although it would greatly improve access to Royal Air Force air displays in the future, the new tube extension was to hasten the inhibiting growth of suburbia that would eventually all but surround the aerodrome.

In the meantime the Royal Air Force continued its programme of modest expansion, albeit on a shoestring budget. In March 1925 the Air Defence of Great Britain had been placed under the control of Air Marshal Sir John Salmond. Included under his command was the newly-created Auxiliary Air Force, which was to be of personal interest to the new Under-Secretary of State for Air, Sir Philip Sassoon. Sir Philip, who had made his first flight with Tom Sopwith in a Blériot at Hendon thirteen years earlier, was to become a leading personality at the aerodrome in the 1930s. As there was now every possibility of the RAF taking over the airfield on a permanent basis, all vestiges of its recent past were being removed. Temporary buildings were demolished and hangars and workshops cleared of unwanted contents including a number of civil aircraft stored on the aerodrome. One of these was the ex-Harry Hawker Sopwith Scooter, G-EACZ, which, having been stored on the site since Hawker's death, was sold in May to C. Clayton who planned to enter it in air races for Dudley 'Dangerous Dan' Watt, a racing pilot of some repute.

By the time the RAF staged its fifth annual pageant, renamed yet again as the Royal Air Force Display, the aerodrome was virtually empty, the only civil operation in residence being the Savage Skywriting concern with its fleet of ex-RAF SE5As.

The Display of 1925 was a thoroughly professional affair with the RAF handling all facets of the organisation, from car parking to catering. The event was again attended by King George V and Queen Mary accompanied by the Duke and Duchess of York. Flt Lt Walter Longton, who by now had built up a large personal following, delighted the crowds with a thrilling aerobatic display in a twin-engined Boulton & Paul Bugle while fending off attacks by two determined CFS Grebes flown by Flg Off J.N. Boothman, and Flt Lt H.A. Hammersley who had recently returned to service flying. There was parachuting from Fairey Fawns, two squadrons of which flew over in formation, while six DH53 Humming Birds, having been ordered by the RAF as liaison aircraft, took part in the HQ race which was won by Wing Commander Sholto Douglas. The Gloster Gamecock, Blackburn Cubbaroo, Hawker Heron and Hedgehog, Bristol Brandon, Short Springbok and the Handley Page Hendon transport were some of the new and experimental types shown. Apart from the spectacular set piece, the bombing of another full-scale mock-up of a ship by

Virginias, Aldershots and Flycatchers, the highlight of the show which was broadcast by the BBC for the first time, was the formation manoeuvring by Gloster Grebes of No 25 Squadron in response to directions given by the King on the ground by radio telephony (R/T).

The 1925 display at Hendon was the last attended by Grahame-White after more than a quarter of a century. His London Flying Club had closed to become part of 400,000 sq ft of the Grahame-White Co Ltd property situated to the south of Airfield Road leased to Standard Telephones & Cable Ltd. Included in the deal was most of the factory space and the Clubhouse which was subsequently turned into laboratories. The golf course was leased to the Colindale Golf Club and the south airfield used for grazing sheep! In view of what he considered as the government's underhanded dealing over the preceeding five years, Claude Grahame-White was now determined to get the best deal he could for his property, however long that should take. However, any sale was complicated by the fact that parts of the Aerodrome remained Grahame-White's personal property while others belonged to his company. Although the charges against his property arising from the wartime production loans had been dropped by the government, the Inland Revenue still demanded outstanding Income Taxes amounting to £41,158.0s.2d owed by the Company plus £11,864.0s.11d personal liability. By the end of the year the Air Ministry had agreed to deduct these amounts from any figure that might be agreed for the sale of the property.

Early in the new year, the last of Grahame-White's aircraft held in storage at Hendon were auctioned off at a sale in one of the Belfast hangars. One of the Bantams was sold to F.G. Miles of Shoreham, soon to begin his own aircraft manufacturing company, but most of the aeroplanes including a number of Boxkites, G-W 1600s and the Ganymedes were sold for scrap. It was widely reported at the time that the final amount paid to Grahame-White for the sale of the London Aerodrome was as much as £500,000, but this was difficult to verify. Although the bulk of the purchase money had been paid by March 1927 the whole protracted and unfortunate affair was not completed until August 1929 by which time London Aerodrome's founder had long since left the country and the aviation industry, to live and work abroad concentrating on his property investments.

However, by 1926 ownership of Hendon Aerodrome had passed to the Air Council and the Royal Air Force not only had a permanent showground at which to stage its flourishing Displays, but had then to decide what the long term future of the airfield should be. While that was being debated, hundreds of RAF personnel moved to Hendon at the beginning of June to prepare for the most important event in the aerial calendar.

The 1926 RAF Air Display was noteworthy for an exciting aerobatic performance by Sqn Ldr R.L.R. Atcherley in a Gamecock, with Virginia and Hyderabad bombers remaining airborne during the whole programme, and the presentation to the King of the four Fairey IIID crews, who had recently completed the first return flight to the Cape. The growing importance of the new and experimental types displayed at Hendon was underlined by the appearance of such revolutionary types as the Cierva Autogiro, hovered by Capt F.T. Courtney, winner of the 1920 Aerial Derby, and the remarkable Pterodactyl flown by Flt Lt J.S. Chick.

The Sprat, Vendace, Gorcock, Hornbill, Avenger, Firefly, Fox, Atlas, Boarhound, Hyena, Vespa, Ava and Argosy were all seen in public for the first, and for many, the last time. Following the spectacular destruction of the set piece, an enemy airfield heavily defended with AA guns, and the return of the bombers having completed their long-distance reliability trials, the show came to an end with the RAF Memorial Fund benefiting by £6,905.

The following weekend, Hendon was again chosen as the venue for the fifth King's Cup Air Race which was won by Hubert Broad in a DH Moth, G-EBMO, at an average speed of 90.4mph. An assortment of powerful Airdisco Martinsydes entered the Race including a Nimbus-powered F4, G-EBKL, which finished in 3rd place at 151.9mph

and a Viper-powered F6, G-EBKK, which failed to start.

Since the creation of the first Auxiliary Air Force Squadrons in August 1925, the Air Ministry had been considering the possibility of using Hendon as a permanent home for the London-based units and on 18 January 1927, No 600 (City of London) Squadron, moved the short distance from Northolt to Hendon Air Station. No 600 Sqn, commanded by the Rt Hon Fred E. Guest MP, was joined by No 601 (County of London) Squadron six months later under the command of Sqn Ldr Lord Edward Grosvenor, an ex-RNAS Blériot pilot. Both AAF squadrons were equipped with DH9A day bombers and Avro 504Ks for training and were placed under the control of the Air Defence of Great Britain Command.

The same Command took over organisation of the RAF Display from 1927 onwards. A Permanent Secretary was also appointed, a permanent new grandstand seating 3,000 spectators was built and a loudspeaker system installed in the public enclosures. On Saturday 2 July, almost 90,000 people braved wind and rain to watch the largest number of aircraft on display at Hendon to date. The King and Queen, the Duke of York and the King of Spain were present in the Royal enclosure to watch individual aerobatics by pairs of Siskins, Gamecocks and the perennial Avro 504s, while No 41 Squadron's Siskins manoeuvred to music relayed

Grahame-White's lavish London Flying Club, with tennis courts and a golf course, located on the south side of Aerodrome Road was opened in 1919.

The luxurious Grahame-White GW E7 five-seater 'Aero Limousine' made its first flight at Hendon in August 1919. Its high cost compared to converted wartime bombers, doomed it to failure.

over the loudspeakers. Formation aerobatics were performed by five Genet Moths flown by pilots of the Central Flying School who included D'Arcy Greig, Stainforth, Atcherley and Waghorn, all of whom were to become household names in the near future. The two resident AAF squadrons joined No 12 (B) Squadron Fairey Foxes in the day-bomber event and attacks on marauding tribesmen surrounding a beleaguered community of European traders were depicted in that year's dramatic set-piece. Notable newcomers of 1927 included an unusually high number of types which eventually saw service with RAF such as the Fairey IIIF, Wapiti, Sidestrand, Hinaidi and the Bristol Bulldog. On 1 December 1927 the Station Headquarters was formed under Wing Commander D.S.K. Creslie. Royal Air Force Station Hendon had become a reality.

The Bristol Bullet that Flight Lieutenant Rollo de Haga Haig flew to second place in the 1921 Aerial Derby.

4 ROYAL AIR FORCE HENDON

From the outset it had been Trenchard's aim to make the Auxiliary Air Force (AAF) a sought-after élite force by restricting membership to only the very best volunteers, an aim enthusiastically endorsed by No 601 (County of London) Squadron's first CO, Lord Edward Grosvenor, who was one of Trenchard's most fervant supporters. Within weeks of moving to Hendon, the Prince of Wales opened 601 Squadron's new Town Headquarters at 54 Kensington Park Road, which quickly became one of the 'Best Clubs in Town' and the squadron earned the nickname of 'The Millionaires' Mob'. Installed in the adjacent Belfast hangar on the east of the airfield was its sister Auxiliary unit and bitter rival, No 600 (City of London) Squadron, which had its Headquarters at Finsbury Barracks and whose pilots were considered by 601 as a 'rather scruffy lot'. However, many of them were experienced wartime pilots now employed in the professions, commerce or even politics. Although two of London's Auxiliary Squadrons were based at Hendon, there was little AAF activity during weekdays. Both units had only a small regular nucleus comprising an adjutant, assistant adjutant and chief flying instructor,

engineer officer and a number of NCO and airmen instructors. The squadrons' flying, which at the time averaged about 1,000 flying hours a year, was restricted to weekends plus one weekday evening during the summer and an annual summer camp.

Nevertheless, movements at Hendon increased substantially during the year as visiting VIPs and senior RAF personnel found RAF Hendon a convenient gateway to London. With its permanent airshow facilities, Hendon was also the favourite venue for numerous official military demonstrations and displays, apart from the annual RAF Display, held for the benefit of foreign dignitaries and visiting Heads of State. One such display in which 150 RAF aircraft took part was attended by King Amanullah and Queen Souriya of Afghanistan on 17 March 1928. Ironically, the RAF put on another very different, although equally impressive, display for the King and Queen when they were deposed nine months later. More than 580 people of various nationalities were evacuated by RAF transport aircraft from European legations in Kabul during disturbances in Afghanistan, flying a total of 57,438 miles over 10,000ft mountains in one of the severest winters on record with the loss of only two aircraft.

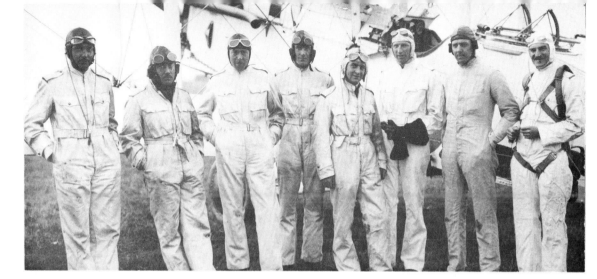

RIGHT: Pilots of 601 Sqn AAF 'The Millionaires' Mob' pose in front of their DH9A at Hendon in 1928. They are, from left to right, Mahoney, Ashley Haward, Bill Thornton, John Parkes, Norman Jones, Nigel Norman, Bill Collett (killed in a crash at Hendon in 1934 when OC of 600 Sqn) and Whitehead Read.

BELOW: An aerial view of RAF Hendon taken on 20 March 1932 showing the AAF squadron's Wapiti IIAs and Avro 504Ns and hangars. The left and centre hangar now form the RAF Museum, while the right hangar was destroyed in World War Two.

In the meantime, Auxiliary flying training from Hendon was not without its incidents. On 6 May, two DH9As belonging to 600 Squadron collided while making a formation approach to the aerodrome. One of the aircraft crashed in Abbey Fields, Mill Hill, its pilot, Plt Off H.O. Young, being fortunate to be dragged clear of the blazing aircraft by trainee Jesuit priests from nearby St Joseph's college.

Six weeks later the two Hendon squadrons took part for the first time in the ninth RAF Air Display in front of record crowds of nearly 100,000 people, the biggest show of air power that had ever been staged in the world at the time. Prominent events on the programme, in which all the aircraft were of post-war manufacture, included a slow flying demonstration by a No 24 Squadron Cirrus Moth flown by Flt Lt D.S. Don; a breathtaking demonstration of 'crazy' flying by Flg Off D.A. Boyle and Sqn Ldr R.L.R. Atcherley, also in Moths; a low-level attack on the airfield by Fairey Foxes of No 12 (Bomber) Squadron and a climb contest by supercharged and unsupercharged Siskin fighters. Virginias, Hyderabads, Foxes, Horsleys and Woodcocks took part in a combined battle for London while Fleet Air Arm Flycatchers, RAF Fairey IIIFs and the AAF DH9As attacked and destroyed the set piece oil refinery. A huge Beardmore Inflexible dominated the new and experimental park while at the other end of the scale the diminutive Halton Minus lightplane made an appearance alongside the exotically-named Partridge, Hawfinch, Wizard and Vickers Vellore. One of the most popular static exhibits was the 1927 Schneider Trophy winning Supermarine S5 floatplane. The 1928 Display, again attended by the King and Queen and Duke of York, as well as no less than six reigning Princes of India, raised more than £10,000 for the RAF Benevolent Fund for the first time.

At what had now become Hendon's second most important spectator event, Wally Hope flew the DH Gipsy Moth to victory in the King's Cup Air Race for the second year running at an increased speed of 105.5mph. A potentially more serious contest took place on the evening of 14 August, when the 'greatest air manoeuvres in history' took place with more than 300 RAF aircraft taking part. 'War' had been declared between 'Eastland', a continental power, and 'Westland', of which London was the capital. 'Enemy' aircraft of Nos 600 and 601 Squadrons made an audacious 'attack' on the Air Ministry and although they were intercepted by the defending forces, they nevertheless claimed success.

No 601 Squadron went on to win the Viscount Esher Trophy for the best all-round unit in the Auxiliary Air Force, for the second year in succession which was presented by the Chief of Air Staff at the end of the year. In the meantime, yet another air display at Hendon, held this time for the benefit of the

Sultan of Muscat and Oman on 14 November, was marred when a Fairey Fox crashed during a demonstration killing the pilot, Flt Lt Somervell and his passenger.

In the early months of 1929 a succession of Very Important Persons used Hendon for the first time. On 26 April, the Prince of Wales flew to Tangmere in Wapiti J9095, belonging to No 24 Squadron flown by Sqn Ldr D.S. Don, while one of the squadron's Fairey IIIF aircraft was used to convey the newly-elected Prime Minister, Ramsay MacDonald, from his constituency near Lossiemouth to Hendon on 20 June. The Prince of Wales was the first member of the Royal Family to make regular use of aircraft as a form of transport as was Ramsay MacDonald the first British Prime Minister so to do.

The RAF Display, held on 13 July, again broke all attendance records with 132,242 counted through the turnstiles. Ironically, the programme was less memorable than in previous years. The highlights being a formation flypast by five Supermarine Southampton flying-boats of No 201 Squadron, an aerobatic formation flight by No 22 Squadron Grebes fitted with the Savage smoke system and a mass parachute jump from Vickers Vimy bombers. The main battle revolved around the set piece, a customs house by a port, with Flycatchers, Fairey IIIFs, Siskins and Hyderabads joining in the action. A mobile W/T trailer was moved in to Hendon for the first time to provide a rudimentary air traffic control during the

Display, but the new and experimental types were noticeable by their absence having been withdrawn in order to appear at the last International Aero Show due to be held at Olympia the following week which included aircraft on order for the RAF and Air Ministry technical exhibits.

Also held during the following week at Hendon was the eighth King's Cup Air Race which was won in convincing style by Sqn Ldr R.L.R. Atcherley flying a two-seat Gloster Grebe at a speed of 150.3mph. Only slightly slower, at 145.32mph, was Capt A.M. Blake in a Blackburn Lincock, but he was placed no higher than tenth overall on handicap. 'Batchy' Atcherley became a national hero when, as part of the RAF's victorious Schneider Trophy Team, he briefly held the world speed record on 12 September with a speed of 370mph over 100 km in a Supermarine S6 over the Solent.

The Prince of Wales made his first flight from Hendon in a private aircraft on 9 August, a DH60M Gipsy Moth G-AAKV, to Berck in France, via Lympne, again with Sqn Ldr Don at the controls. Three weeks later, the Prince took delivery of his own Gipsy Moth, registered G-AALG, the first aircraft to be owned by a member of the Royal Family.

August, however, was a month of mixed fortunes for the AAF Squadrons based at Hendon. On the 18th, No 601 Squadron's Commanding Officer, Lord Edward Grosvenor, popularly known as Ned, died suddenly at the early age of thirty-seven. He was replaced by his old friend, Sir Philip Sassoon, who at the time was still the Under-Secretary of State for Air.

Both Auxiliary Squadrons at Hendon were in the process of re-equipping with Westland Wapiti bombers and DH 60M Moth trainers, and on 5 October Flg Off D.A. Boyle was appointed assistant adjutant to 601 Squadron. One of his main pre-occupations over the next few years would be to teach his Commanding Officer to fly. Boyle was later asked if he had been successful. 'I'm not teaching him to fly,' he commented 'only to land.'

Prince George, a frequent visitor to the RAF Displays, made his first flight to Hendon from Smith's Lawn in Windsor Great Park on 10 October in 24 Squadron's 'Royal' Wapiti J9095. On the same day, the Prince of Wales flew out of Hendon in his Moth en route for Sandwich. By the end of the year the two Princes had flown in or out of Hendon on no less than forty-four occasions.

Marshal of the Royal Air Force, Sir Hugh Trenchard, who had been Chief of the Air Staff since 1919, was succeeded in December by Air Chief-Marshal Sir John Salmond, an energetic advocate of air defence, prior to being elevated to the peerage in the 1930 New Year's Honours List.

During the coming year, the number of units based at Hendon was to double. On 17 March No 604 (County of Middlesex) Squadron was formed at Hendon under the Command of Squadron Leader Alan Dore, DSO, equipped initially with DH9A and Avro 504N aircraft. In the first year of its formation the squadron received more than one hundred and fifty applicants for entry as pilots, of whom only fifteen were chosen after interviews with the CO and the adjutant, Flt Lt F.J. Fogarty, a display pilot of note. There was also a long waiting list with all three of Hendon's AAF Squadrons for airmen who had to wait for months in order to be allowed the privilege of putting on overalls and spending their spare time cleaning oil trays and scrubbing hangar floors. No 604 Squadron Town Centre was the Heathrow House, a fine Georgian building behind Jack Straw's Castle on Hampstead Heath, which was opened by the newly-created Lord Trenchard. Most of the pilots were businessmen and who rapidly became known collectively as the 'The Brains Trust'.

Meanwhile 600 Squadron had hosted a visit by Admiral Moffett USN, the first Chief of the US Navy's Bureau of Aeronautics, who was invited to fly one of the squadron's Wapiti aircraft on 28 March. A few weeks later, the Wapitis escorted their Commanding Officer, Sqn Ldr the Hon. Freddie Guest M.P., on the first leg of his flight to East Africa in his own Junkers F13 monoplane. Guest also owned a two-seat Southern Martlet biplane which was available to his squadron pilots, on occasions such as the Annual Camp. Not to be

Fairey Foxes of 12 Squadron prepare to take-off for their display slot in the 1929 RAF Display at Hendon.

No 3 Squadron Bristol Bulldogs are manhandled by their ground crews in the crowded aircraft park at Hendon during the 1929 RAF Display.

outdone by his rivals, Sir Philip Sassoon acquired a Spartan three-seater Mk 1 and a Gipsy Moth. Both these aircraft were almost written-off in one incident. John Gillan, the Squadron's Adjutant had borrowed the Moth from Port Lympne, one of Sir Philip's many charming houses, in order to be back in Hendon that night. By the time he arrived at his destination it was dark and he managed to hit one of the numerous cows belonging to a local farmer, which were allowed to graze on the airfield overnight. The following morning, Flt Lt Brian Thynne, who had previously borrowed the Spartan to fly to his parents' house in Sussex, arrived at Hendon and was so amused at the Moth's predicament that he decided to land close by to get a better look. Unfortunately the Spartan possessed no brakes and ran into the rear of the stricken Moth breaking the Spartan's propeller. Sir Philip was slightly put out by the damage to his aircraft but when Thynne explained, with some affront, that the Moth had reversed into the Spartan, he was so amused that he paid for the damage to both aircraft.

Larger-than-life personalities at Hendon were not restricted to aircrew, for amongst 601 Squadron's 'erks' was one Nevil Shute, and a Corporal T. Wewege Smith who promptly left to join the Foreign Legion from which he soon escaped and returned to face a charge of desertion. He received nothing worse than a severe reprimand for this escapade and a few years later volunteered to become a gunner with the Bolivian Air Force during the Chaco War. Another exotic character to make frequent visits to RAF Hendon, before his death in a motorcycle accident in 1935, was Leading Aircraftman Shaw (Lawrence of Arabia).

Because of a substantial increase in VIP traffic at Hendon — Ramsay MacDonald made the first of six flights of the year from the airfield to Lossiemouth on 6 April in a No 24 Sqn Fairey IIIF — it was decided that another Royal Air Force communications unit would return to the Station after an absence of more than ten years. The Home Communications Flight was created at the beginning of the year equipped with an assortment of aircraft including Genet Moths, Gipsy Moth, Siskins and a Grebe. The Flight also looked after sundry visiting aircraft such as Sir Sefton Brancker's DH Moth, G-EDCA.

The RAF Display had by this time become a very professional affair administered by a permanent staff under Air Commodore B.C.H. Drew (Retd), and although some of the early personalities were no longer involved, Walter Longton having been killed in an air race and Rollo de Haga Haig having retired, the event had earned an enviable reputation for its smooth organisation and prompt timing. A full dress rehearsal was held on the day before the Display, which was attended by thousands of school children from all over North London, and the 1930

Display, held on Saturday 28 June, proved one of the best to date.

The sight of three flights of three Siskins of No 43 Squadron performing formation aerobatics tied together by rubber ropes was declared 'the most excellent performance of the day'. No 600 Squadron's Wapiti formation won high praise for its accuracy and station-keeping while Flg Off Campbell and Plt Off F. Whittle of No 2FTS thrilled the crowds with their crazy flying routine in Avro 504Ns. Flg Off G. de Havilland (RAF Reserve) won the HQ race in a DH60M Moth designed by his father, and CFS pilots flew an inverted formation of Moths. One of the highlights of the day for the 150,000 crowd was the sight of the giant R101 airship flying slowly over the airfield, piloted by Major G.H. Scott, and bowing to King George and Queen Mary in the Royal enclosure. Another formation of RAF flying-boats from Calshot made an impressive flypast while the set piece featured a band of pirates being captured and taken away by a flight of Vickers Vernon transports.

The New and experimental Park was again a feature at Hendon with such types as the revolutionary slotted Handley Page Gugnunc, Vickers 150, Fairey Firefly II, Blackburn Lincock, Bristol Bullpup, DH77 Interceptor, and the Hawker Hart on show. Two of Britain's 1929 Schneider Trophy competitors, the victorious Supermarine S6

and the unsuccessful Gloster VI were included in the static display.

New types were also being based at Hendon. The prototype Hawker Tomtit trainer, J9772, was delivered to the Home Communication Flight and used by the Prince of Wales for a flight to Castle Bromwich on 25 July. A few days later, the Prince took delivery of a brand new DH80A Puss Moth, G-ABBS, which was flown via Hendon to Smith's Lawn by his newly-appointed personal pilot, Flt Lt E.H. Fielden. On 29 July, the Prince of Wales was again at Hendon, destined for Brussels in No 24 Squadron's VIP Fairey IIIF K1115 and on 13 August, he used the same aircraft to visit several RAF units taking part in national exercises up and down the country. At the same time, his younger brother Prince Henry also purchased a DH60M Gipsy Moth, G-ABDB, having recently become the third member of the Royal Family, after Prince Albert the Duke of York, and the Prince of Wales himself, to fly solo.

On 5 October the country was shocked by the news that the R101 airship, so recently seen over Hendon, had crashed near Beauvais in France during an attempt to fly to India via Egypt. The airship had struck a hillside and burst into flames. Forty-seven of fifty-four passengers and crew on board perished in the disaster including Lord Thomson, Secretary of State for Air, and Air Marshal Sir Sefton Brancker. The result of the official inquiry into the accident would ultimately lead to the abandonment of all airship construction in Great Britain for nearly half a century. However, the disaster did little to dim the Prince of Wales' enthusiasm for flying and aeroplanes and on 12 November he flew from Hendon to Calshot in a Saro Cloud amphibian G-ABCJ flown by Flt Lt Scott. The Prince's first landing on water was undertaken in order to visit the giant Dornier Do X flying-boat that was moored at Southampton during a protracted sales tour.

The new year saw increased activity by Hendon's 'weekend flyers'. The AAF squadrons' weekend camps were held throughout the summer months and ever since Flt Lt Gillan, Adjutant of 601 Squadron, made the first night flight by an Auxiliary Air Force aircraft from Hendon in a Moth guided by headlights and flares, it became the fashionable thing to do — providing the weather was good. Apart from Flt Lt 'Joe' Fogarty crashing one of 601's Wapitis, J9096, onto the roof of a house in Hampstead in February, suffering nothing worse than damaged pride, the only real trouble came from the local churches which, not unnaturally, were not impressed by the roar of aircraft taking off and circling at rooftop level drowning the first lesson at Sunday matins. This difficulty was eventually solved by an order that all aircraft were to be airborne and away from the Hendon area by 1045 hours each Sunday and remain away until 1230 hours. As all officers were required to wear uniforms at weekends, the extra time required to change into flying kit caused a number of flights to get away within minutes of the church doors closing.

VIP flights from Hendon were unaffected by such restrictions and were operated as and when required. The Prime Minister made yet another flight to Lossiemouth in the 24 Squadron Fairey IIIF on 1 April, returning to Hendon on the 13th in a record time of 3hr 10min. Between 9-12 May, the Prince of Wales accompanied by Prince George, had flown in his Puss Moth from Hendon — Birmingham — Manchester — Hendon. By the end of the month Flt Lt Fielden moved the Prince's growing fleet of aircraft, comprising two Gipsy Moths and a Puss Moth, from Northolt to Hendon. The Royal aircraft, all of which were finished in the red and blue colours of the Brigade of Guards, were accommodated in the Home Communication Flight's hangar situated on the west side of the airfield and were maintained by H.A. Jenkins and R.T. Hussey, both civilian mechanics who were later given the rank of Flight Sergeant. Politicians continued to favour Hendon for overseas departures in preference to No 24 Squadron's base at Northolt situated some eight miles to the west. On 21 June the new Director of Civil Aviation, Lieutenant-Colonel Francis Shelmerdine was flown from Hendon to Zagreb (Czechoslovakia) by Flt Lt J.G.D. Armour, soon to become Air Equerry to the Prince of Wales, in a Fairey IIIF and returned on the 29th in the same aircraft.

Two days before the Director's return to England, the twelfth Royal Air Force Display had been staged, attracting yet another record crowd of some 170,000. Of the eighteen events on the 1931 programme, emphasis was given to the latest technical innovations including a demonstration of aerial refuelling by two Vickers Virginias and a catapulted take-off by another Virginia. No 43 Squadron, having very recently re-equipped with the new Hawker Fury, made a welcome return to Hendon while 12 Squadron showed off yet another newcomer from the same stable, the speedy Hart light bomber. A formation of No 17 Squadron Bulldogs was joined in the air over the airfield by the three resident AAF squadrons including 604 Squadron flying its new Wapitis for the first time. A spectacular aerobatic demonstration was performed by two Gamecocks flown by Flt Lt M.M. Day and Plt Off D.R.S. Bader and Flt Lt Basil Embry led a flight of five inverted CFS Gipsy Moths. New types shown for the first time, apart from the Hawker Fury which was already in service, were the Short Gurnard, an amphibious fleet fighter, the Gloster SS19, Fairey Gordon, Armstrong Whitworth XVI and Hawker Hoopoe.

As the show drew to a close, Prince Henry Duke of Gloucester, left by air in 24 Squadron's VIP Fairey IIIF. The same aircraft was used by the Prime Minister for his return to Hendon from Berlin on 29 July, when he was escorted from Germany by two more of the Squadron's Fairey IIIFs.

Two new DH80 Puss Moths took up residence at Hendon during September. G-ABRR, the second of its type to be purchased by the Prince of Wales, followed by an American-owned example, serial No 8877, for use by the United States Naval Attaché in London, thus starting a long association with the US Navy and RAF Station Hendon.

In November, Flt Lt S.B. Collett, son of the Lord Mayor of London — one of the original 'Millionaires Mob' — took leave of No 601 Squadron to move across to the neighbouring hangar to take up his appointment as Commanding Officer of No 600 Squadron. At the end of the year Sir Philip Sassoon felt that the pressure of work as Under-Secretary of State of Air required him to reluctantly step down from command of No 601 and hand over to Squadron Leader Sir Nigel Norman.

In spite of the fact that most aircraft manufacturing in the Hendon area had long since ceased, it was reported in December that Mr Lowe-Wylde was testing a BAC Hydroglider on the nearby Welsh Harp reservoir close to where Mr Martin and Mr Handasyde built and tested their unsuccessful monoplane twenty-three years earlier; the BAC Hydroglider proved similarly unsuccessful.

With economic decline threatening most of Europe, the forces were an obvious target for deep cuts in government spending. On 2 February 1932, the Rt Hon Arthur Henderson MP, leader of the Labour Party, opened the League of Nations Disarmament Conference at Geneva and after five years of slow and cautious expansion, the Air Estimates announced in March showed a reduction of almost ten per cent over the previous year, once again bringing the long term future of the service into doubt. However, there were as yet no restrictions to flying at RAF Hendon where the Auxiliary squadrons had almost doubled their flying hours by the end of 1931. Weather, and the notorious Hendon fog in particular, was the only limiting factor.

Nor was there any limit to RAF flying when it came to impressing visiting overseas Heads of State who were judged sympathetic to Great Britain's cause and who were invited to Hendon for demonstrations of the Air Force's latest warplanes and often given an opportunity to fly in some of them. Emir Faisal of Arabia was treated to a local flight in one of No 24 Squadron's Fairey IIIFs on 13 May following an air show put on for his benefit. The main event of Hendon's calendar, however, remained the RAF Display that took place as usual on the last Saturday in June. Despite excellent weather throughout the day, attendance and gross takings were down on previous years — a reflection

K2568 was the first DH60T Tiger Moth I to be delivered to No 24 Squadron at Hendon in 1932.

of the prevailing economic climate. Although the numbers were down, traffic congestion around Hendon was such that New Scotland Yard's Traffic Department requested that the Air Ministry provide aircraft fitted with Radio Telephony to communicate with Police Mobile vehicles and motorcycles. Two Armstrong Whitworth Atlas aircraft of No 2 (AC) Squadron were chosen to become Britain's first aerial traffic spotters and one of them was instrumental in rescuing the Prince of Wales and his party, who were in danger of being late for the opening ceremony, from a traffic jam. The programme featured a slow aeroplane race for DH Tiger Moths, the RAF's new trainer, three No 24 Squadron Fairey IIIFs flying past towing gliders, and a Hart giving two Furies the run-around in the ever popular 'dogfight' event. Hendon's three Auxiliary Squadrons flew over the airfield in an impressive formation making up the letters A A F and no less than six bomber squadrons were dispatched to destroy the set piece enemy aerodrome and fort. The Cierva Autogiro, Pterodactyl and Gugnunc made up an unlikely formation of experimental types while new types on show included Hawkers' Osprey and Nimrod, the Tiger Moth, Wallace, Vildebeest, Jockey and the Bristol 120 turreted fighter. Two new heavy bombers from Handley Page and Fairey, the Heyford and the Hendon respectively, made their debuts.

Most of the new and experimental types remained at Hendon after the Display to be exhibited at the first SBAC (Society of British Aircraft Manufacturers) Show held at the airfield on Monday 27 June. A total of thirty-one aircraft, including a few sundry civil machines, were on show to potential buyers and foreign guests, including the Italian Minister of Aviation, General Balbo, with each company given eight minutes in which to demonstrate its product. Visitors were given flights in some of the aircraft after the Show from which the Press was excluded. In view of the interest generated by the Show the SBAC decided to make it an annual event.

The Prince of Wales continued his close association with the aerodrome despite making an extensive two month tour of Europe during the autumn. On his return, he presented the Lord Esher Trophy to 604 Squadron for the first time and by the end of the year replaced one of his Puss Moths with a new four-seater DH83 Fox Moth, G-ACDD.

Sir Philip Sassoon flew out of Hendon on 10 January in a 24 Squadron Fairey IIIF bound for Le Bourget and a few weeks later his old squadron, No 601, together with 600, began to re-equip with Hawker Hart day-bombers. Unfortunately, it was during a practice formation dive of 601's new Harts in May that the squadron suffered its first casualties. The formation, led by the Adjutant, was late in pulling out of a dive and one of the Harts crashed

on the airfield and caught fire, killing the pilot Plt Off the Viscount Knebworth, and his observer L.A.C. Harrison. Another aircraft in the formation, flown by Flt Lt Brian Thynne, touched the ground during the pull-out, fortunately without serious damage.

Other new aircraft delivered to Hendon during the month included Sir Philip Sassoon's Percival Gull IV G-ACGR, and the first twin-engined addition to the Prince of Wales' growing fleet, a twelve-seater Vickers Viastra X G-ACCC. On 16 May the Prince flew back to Hendon from Cardiff aboard the new aircraft to present the Esher Trophy to No 604 Squadron for the second year in succession. The occasion was attended by several

Mill Hill schoolboys who were fortunate to be given flights in the squadron's aircraft. The next day, Captain A. Eden, Under-Secretary of State for Foreign Affairs, left Hendon for Geneva to attend the Disarmament Conference. At the time, there was still considerable optimism that the conference would lead to a lasting peace in Europe and pacifism was again in fashion. Several Peace Councils had been established in Great Britain, including one in Hendon where the local Branch campaigned vigorously against military spending of any sort, and on the RAF Display in particular.

However, in spite of some local opposition and the bad weather, the show went on as usual. A formation of Singapore, Southampton and Saro

A selection of aircraft at Hendon in 1932 with a visiting Hawker Hart I, K1426, of 12 Squadron in the foreground, and an Avro 504N and two Westland Wapiti IIAs of 601 Squadron AAF in the background.

Cloud flying-boats, well suited to the wet weather, flew over the airfield while Demons, Audaxes and Wapitis kept the damp crowds entertained with supply dropping and formation flying. One of 24 Squadron's veteran Avro 504Ns took part in the Balloon bursting event and three flights of three No 25 Squadron Furies performed a tied-together aerobatic routine that had taken five months to perfect. In spite of the low cloud and almost continuous rain, only one item on the programme, a mass flypast by three bomber squadrons, had to be

cancelled. However, in the adverse conditions, one of the traffic-spotting Atlas aircraft was mistaken for a Sidestrand bomber and 'attacked' by two Siskins taking part in the 'dog-fight' event. As the Atlas beat a hasty retreat it lost its way in the low cloud and being low on fuel was forced to land in a field near Finchley.

Two record breakers, the Vickers Vespa and the Fairey Monoplane, height and distance respectively, were on static display in the rain alongside several new types including the Super Fury, the Blackburn

An aerial view of the 'New Type' park at the 1932 RAF Display. In the foreground are the Heyford and Hendon bomber prototypes and a Tiger Moth. Others include the Osprey and Nimrod, Wildebeest and the Bristol 120 turreted fighter.

Torpedo Bomber, the Armstrong-Whitworth XVI and the Gloster Gauntlet. The latter, along with a larger selection of new types, was flown by Howard Saint at the second SBAC Display at Hendon two days later, this time under cloudless blue skies. During the afternoon, the Prince of Wales' latest acquisition, a twin-engine DH84 Dragon G-ACGG, flew in from Holbrook.

As more and more of the RAF's VIP and communications flights were originating at Hendon, the Air Ministry eventually decided to transfer No 24 Squadron to Hendon from Northolt on 9 July. The Squadron absorbed the Home Communications Flight and formed three flights, HQ, A & B, while C Flight remained at Northolt as a Station Flight under the command of Flt Lt H.A. Hammersley MC. With the Squadron came a mixed fleet of Fairey IIIFs, Harts, Gipsy Moths, a solitary Bulldog and Tomtit K1782. The latter was subsequently used during the autumn of 1933 to give Lord Londonderry, the Secretary of State for Air, an intensive course of flying instruction.

One of the most significant events of the year, however, was Germany, now led by Adolf Hitler, walking out of the Disarmament Conference at Geneva. Suddenly pacifism was out of fashion and there were immediate calls by Members of Parliament, the forces and industrialists for Britain to re-arm without delay. One of the most vociferous advocates of re-armament during this period was

Rear Admiral Sir Murray Sueter MP. In a speech to the House of Lords on 29 November, Lord Londonderry declared that 'our present relative weakness in the air cannot be allowed to continue'. At the time, Britain's defences rested with thirteen Royal Air Force squadrons — eight equipped with Bulldogs, three with Furies and two with Demons. The 1934 Air Estimates introduced in March gave little indication of any extensive re-armament. Although the amount of money requested was up slightly on the previous year, this was due in the main to an increased appropriation for the Fleet Air Arm. However, the Prime Minister, Stanley Baldwin, assured the House that 'if the Disarmament Conference failed, steps would be taken to bring about an Air-Disarmament Convention; if that failed, the Government would

RIGHT: A tight formation of 19 Squadron Bristol Bulldogs, led by Flt Lt Harry Broadhurst, trailing smoke perform a formation loop over Hendon watched by a Gaumont-British News camera crew during the 1934 RAF Display.

BELOW: The Prince of Wales arrives at the 1934 RAF Display in his Vickers Viastra X G-ACCC flying over the Supermarine Type 224, K2890, and a Hawker Fury in the 'New Type' park.

proceed to bring the strength of our Air Force up to the strength of the strongest Air Force within striking distance of this country'.

While politicians once again pondered the future of the services, life at RAF Station Hendon had settled to a busy routine. In addition to having four active squadrons in residence, and the Prince of Wales' fleet, now comprising the Viastra and the Dragon — the Gipsy Moth, Puss Moth and Fox Moth having been part exchanged for the latter — the station played host to several members of overseas Royalty. The Viastra in particular was heavily utilised during the spring of 1934. On 8 March, Prince Axel of Denmark was conveyed to Speke and on the following day the same aircraft was buzzed by a playful RAF Bulldog near Hindhead while returning to Hendon from Portsmouth with the Prince of Wales aboard. The playful pilot was later severely reprimanded. Flt Lt 'Mouse' Fielden was the pilot on both occasions and was again at the controls when the Prince arrived at Hendon in the Viastra to open the fifteenth RAF Display on 30 June to the delight of the 136,000 spectators.

The programme, although predictable, provided spectacular entertainment with such events as synchronized aerobatics by Furies of Nos 25 and 43 Squadrons, close formation aerobatics by No 19 Squadron Bulldogs trailing smoke — led by Flt Lt Harry Broadhurst who later stated that 'Hendon was the only RAF airfield over which pilots were ordered to fly low', and an unusual formation of RAF Rota autogiros. The CFS Instructors' inverted formation was performed by Avro Tutors for the first time and the now familiar flying-boat formation consisted of a Singapore II, a Scapa, the Short R23/31, a Blackburn Perth and three Saro Clouds.

However, it was during the flypast of three Auxiliary squadrons that one of No 600 Squadron's Harts suffered an engine failure with tragic results. As the pilot attempted to turn back towards the airfield the Hart stalled and crashed, catching fire on impact. Neither of the crew was critically injured but while the pilot was able to get clear of the burning aircraft, Sqn Ldr S.B. Collett, 600 Squadron's commanding officer, was trapped in the observer's cockpit when his parachute snagged on the Scarff ring and he died in the flames despite the efforts of the part-time RAF fire crew. Although the show went on, including the ritual destruction of the set piece by waves of bombers, the event was rather overshadowed by the first fatal accident to occur in the series of Hendon Displays.

During the summer of 1934 the political situation in Europe deteriorated further. Baldwin's Air Disarmament Conference had failed and Germany resigned from the League of Nations. However, Britain's aircraft industry began to grasp the reality of the situation, even if the politicians did not, by gearing itself up for a period of rapid military expansion. On the Monday following the RAF

Display, the SBAC held its second Show at Hendon with no less than thirty-nine exhibits, several of which had already been seen by the public two days earlier including two of the main contenders for the Air Ministry's F7/30 intercepter specification, the Supermarine 225 and Westland's four-gun fighter.

Only two weeks later, the Government announced that 500 new aircraft would be ordered for the RAF and on their return from annual camp, Hendon's three AAF units were re-categorised as fighter squadrons with 604 Squadron exchanging its

A 24 Squadron Hawker Hart I VII transport, K3001 one of a number of Harts based at RAF Hendon during the mid-1930s.

The first DH89 to be delivered to the RAF in 1935, K5070 served with 24 Squadron at Hendon for Air Council work.

ageing DH4As for Harts, although 600 Squadron had to wait until the following January before replacing its Wapitis with the new type. Another new aircraft that would remain a familiar sight at Hendon over the next decade was the DH89 Dragon Rapide, a twin-engined six-seat biplane developed from the Dragon. The first of the type to be ordered by the RAF as a VIP transport was delivered to No 24 Squadron on 29 March 1935 and ten days later, the Prime Minister, Ramsay MacDonald, and his Foreign Secretary, Sir John Simon, flew to Paris in the new aircraft to ratify an agreement whereby Great Britain and France 'should undertake immediately to give the assistance of their Air Forces to whichever of them might be the victim of unprovoked aerial aggression'.

A second Dragon Rapide, G-ACTT, arrived at Hendon from Smith's Lawn, Windsor on 27 April. The Prince of Wales sold both the Viastra and the Dragon and replaced them with a pair of Rapides, the second of which, G-ADDD, was delivered in June. By this time a self-contained suite of rooms had been built on to the RAF Mess at Hendon for the exclusive use of the Prince of Wales and his personal guests. The suite was accessible from the 'Royal' hangar and afforded complete privacy for anyone using it. One of the Prince's friends, Mrs Wallace Simpson, later the Duchess of Windsor, is said to have stayed in the suite on a number of occasions during this period.

On 22 May the Government had announced proposals for further considerable expansion of the RAF. By March 1937 the strength of the RAF based at home (exclusive of the Fleet Air Arm) would reach 1,500 first-line aircraft. This figure compared with the mid-1935 strength of 580 aircraft and with the total of 840 which was to have been reached by March 1937, under the programme of July 1934. Three days later the first Empire Air Day Celebration, in aid of the RAF Benevolent Fund, was held at selected RAF

Stations, including Hendon. The resident squadrons were opened to the public, and their aircraft displayed on the ground and in the air. Fourteen thousand people attended. The event was a useful dress rehearsal for the RAF Display held on the last Saturday of June, the highlight of which was to be a mass flypast of seventy-nine aircraft from nine squadrons. The 1935 Display was the first not to feature a set piece although most of the old favourites were included in a programme which again was not without incident. For the second consecutive year an accident occurred in full view of the public when a CFS Tutor crashed

The first of two DH89 Dragon Rapides purchased by the Prince of Wales and operated by 'The Royal Flight' at RAF Hendon from April 1935.

during the crazy flying routine. Although the aircraft was completely wrecked, the hapless pilot, Flg Off I.V. Hue Williams, was able to walk away with no more than his pride hurt. No 19 Squadron made a return appearance performing formation aerobatics in their recently delivered Gloster Gauntlets and Flg Off A.J. Pegg demonstrated the DH88 Comet, winner of the previous year's London to Melbourne Air Race. New types seen for the first time were the Supermarine Seagull amphibian, the Vincent, Vickers Type 207 torpedo bomber, Armstrong-Whitworth 23 trooper, and Gloster's four-gun fighter, the Gladiator. The latter, flown by Flt Lt P.E.G. Sayer, was the star of the third SBAC Show on 1 July which attracted forty exhibits. On the same day the Duke and

Duchess of York made their first flight together having boarded a four-engine DH86 at Hendon bound for Brussels, to attend the Great Exhibition, with an escort of six RAF fighters.

Immediately prior to the Display, 604 Squadron became the first Auxiliary Squadron to re-equip with the Hawker Demon, a fighter version of the Hart. Within weeks of the type's introduction, one of the squadron's aircraft was involved in a fatal accident when Demon K4502 crashed on to a railway line close to the Colindale Underground Station on 4 August killing the crew, Flg Off R.L. Nimmo and AC2 S.J. Mabbut.

During the year, some of the last reminders of Hendon's early post-war period finally disappeared. The Savage Skywriting Company, the only civil

A Savage Skywriting Co SE5A G-EBIB, built by Wolseley in 1918, was based at Hendon in the 1920s and is now preserved in the Science Museum.

operator to be based at RAF Hendon, finally closed its doors and the fleet of vintage SE5As was disposed of. Although the company was no more, the name 'SAVAGE SKYWRITING' painted in large white letters on the doors and roofs of its hangars was to remain a familiar landmark for pilots for a number of years. The Auxiliary squadrons on the other side of the airfield used them to check if the weather was good enough for flying. If they could read the letters they flew, otherwise they stayed on the ground.

On the other side of Aerodrome Road, the former London Flying Club was taken over by the Metropolitan Police School, created by Viscount Trenchard who had become Commissioner of the Metropolitan Police in 1931. With the political situation in Europe worsening by the month — Germany had re-introduced conscription earlier in the year, the civil war in Austria continued and in October, Italy invaded Abyssinia — No 24 Squadron was kept busy shuttling Government ministers to and fro between the capitals of Europe, and ferrying Air Council Members to defence bases within Great Britain. On 13 December Air Commodore A.W. Tedder, Director of Training, was conveyed from Hendon to Desford and back in one of the squadron's Rapides flown by Flt Lt R.R. Nash. A month later an additional 'C' Flight was added to the squadron's establishment with Nash as flight commander. He was also Sir Philip Sassoon's personal pilot and instructor, having taken over this

protracted task from Dermot Boyle who had been posted to India. Rupert Nash was one of a select band of Hendon personalities during the 1930s. He had a habit of making inverted approaches to the airfield when flying the Hart and rolling-out as he crossed the main railway line on finals — without VIPs in the back — and on the occasion when Sassoon phoned him from Cranwell to tell him that he had just soloed, Nash asked about the condition of the aeroplane. Sassoon was reported to have replied 'The aeroplane — oh that, dear boy, is confetti'.

On 20 January 1936 King George V passed away peacefully in his sleep at Sandringham and at 1125hrs the following day King Edward VIII, the former Prince of Wales, boarded his Rapide G-ADDD at Bircham Newton accompanied by his brother the Duke of York for the fifty-five minute flight to Hendon — the first made by a reigning British Monarch. The new reign began against a background of growing political turmoil. Italian troops had already occupied most of Abyssinia and in March Hitler's forces moved into the Rhineland, in violation of the Treaty of Versailles. In response to these threatening developments, the Air Estimates for 1936-7 were almost twice as much as the previous year and made provisions for the establishment of 123 squadrons for the Home Defence Force with a front-line strength of 1,500 aircraft.

A number of new Auxiliary Air Force squadrons had been formed at the beginning of the year; one of which, No 610 (City of Chester) Squadron benefitted from a close liaison with 600 Squadron which provided aircraft and instructors during the initial work-up period at Hooton Park. All three of Hendon's AAF units were on display to the public for the second Empire Air Day on 23 May and a week later Flt Lt Lord Carlow and Plt Off R.G. Kellett flew 600 Squadron's first night cross-country sortie from Hendon to Heston in a Tiger Moth. The Squadron's Harts also featured in the set piece attack at the seventeenth Royal Air Force Display, participating with No 604's Demons in the air drill event.

The 1936 Display was the largest yet staged at Hendon and would be remembered for the varied number of new types in the static park. Apart from the regular favourites, without which no Hendon Display would have been complete — formation aerobatics, dog-fights, crazy flying and skittle bombing — a selection of 'Historic' types was featured for the first time; a Sopwith Camel, a Wright biplane, a Blériot, a Caudron and a Farman 'Horace' amongst them, all of which were in marked contrast to the latest products on offer from Britain's rapidly expanding aero industry. Prototypes of the Spitfire, Hurricane, Wellington, Whitley, Battle and Lysander were just a few of the soon-to-be-famous names that made their public debut at Hendon on 27 June 1936.

Over the years, the RAF Displays had earned an unrivalled reputation for spectacle, split-second timing, and expert crowd control — nearly 170,000 people and more than 20,000 cars attended the 1936 Display, all marshalled through a total of eight exits by hundreds of RAF police, Metropolitan police and RAC patrolmen. All the flying events were meticulously practised and rehearsed for months prior to the show. Participating pilots were issued with spotless white flying overalls for the occasion and the whole event, inevitably held under clear blue skies, rivalled Wimbledon, held in the same week, Ascot, and even the Test Match as a social attraction for the rich and famous who once again flocked to Hendon in their droves on the last Saturday of June.

On 8 July King Edward, again accompanied by the Duke of York, left Hendon on the first leg of a tour of inspection of Northolt, Wittering and Martlesham Heath RAF Stations in the Rapide, and two weeks later the King's Flight was officially formed with the newly-promoted Wing Commander Fielden as its first Captain. The Air Ministry had agreed to finance Royal aircraft and their support, which would remain the responsibility of No 24 Squadron. The fleet, which at the time comprised a single Dragon Rapide, the other G-ACTT having been sold earlier in the year, was accommodated in one of the squadron's hangars adjacent to the Officers'

Mess at Hendon, henceforward to be called the King's Hangar.

During the last week of July air exercises were carried out to give collective defence training to squadrons of the Metropolitan Air Force including AAF units that at the time were at their annual camps; No 600 Squadron was at Hawkinge, Kent, 601 at Lympne and 604 at North Weald. For the first time it was assumed that attacking forces would come in over the seaboard of south-eastern England. On their return to Hendon, all three AAF squadron's began replacing the long serving Avro 504Ns with Tutors and 601 received the first of its Demons. In November the approved version of the latter squadron's badge was signed by King Edward VIII and presented to the CO, Sqn Ldr Brian Thynne, by his predecessor, the Rt Hon Sir Philip Sassoon. No 604 Squadron's crest, a scimitar with the motto 'If you want peace, prepare for war', was also one of the few official badges to be approved by Edward VIII before his dramatic abdication in favour of the Duke of York on 11 December.

As a result of RAF Station Hendon, and its four squadrons, transferring from Bomber Command to Fighter Command on 1 December, No 600 (F) Squadron began re-equipping with Hawker Demons early in the New Year.

The international situation was showing no sign of improving. Germany had formed an Axis with Italy and civil war had broken out in Spain involving men and weapons from Italy, Germany and the Soviet Union. The 1937 Air Estimates introduced to Parliament in March were again double the amount of the previous year and called for the establishment of no less than 100 squadrons at Home and twenty-six overseas. Winston Churchill, now a backbencher, was again in the forefront of the re-armament faction in Parliament. He had already made his position clear in a recent speech on the subject stating that 'The only real security upon which sound military principles will rely is that you should be master of your own air', and in the House he deplored the London County Council's decision announced in April to ban local cadet corps and school children from attending the RAF Display dress rehearsal traditionally held on the Friday preceeding the event.

May was again a busy period at the airfield heralded by the delivery of a new aircraft for the King's Flight. The new King, George VI, had retained Fielden's services as Captain of the King's Flight, but as the Dragon Rapide was the personal property of the former King, it was sold to Western Airways in March, temporarily leaving the flight without an aircraft. However, on Fielden's recommendation an Airspeed Envoy Mk III was selected and purchased by the Air Ministry and the aircraft, G-AEXX was officially allotted to No 24 Squadron for use by the King's Flight on 7 May. Initially the Envoy was for the sole use of the

One of the new types shown at the last RAF Display held on 26 June 1937, was the DH93 Don trainer prototype. The type was later to serve with 24 Squadron at Hendon as a light transport.

Displayed in the 1937 RAF Display 'Historic Type' park was Bristol F.2b F4587 which was issued to 24 Squadron on 19 January 1937 for display purposes. It was later destroyed by enemy action while held in storage at Hendon.

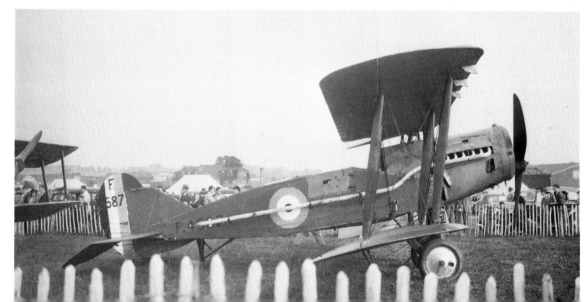

monarch and his family while other members of the Royal Family were flown in 24 Squadron's VIP aircraft such as the Dragon Rapide in which the Duke of Kent flew from Hendon to Yatebury on 27 May. On a sadder note, the Hon F.E. Guest, No 600 Squadron's first Honorary Air Commodore died suddenly in May, and at his request his ashes were scattered over the Welsh Harp, which had always been considered a life-line to pilots heading to Hendon in bad weather, from one of the Squadron's Demons at dusk on 22 May.

Within days, Guest's great friend and colleague, Sir Philip Sassoon announced that he was standing down as Under-Secretary of State for Air due to ill-health, to be succeeded by Lieutenant-Colonel A.J. Muirhead, but would retain his position as Honorary Commodore of No 601 Squadron. A month later the RAF Coronation Display, under the command of Air Chief-Marshal Sir Hugh Dowding, took place under clear blue skies in front of HM King George VI, Queen Elizabeth and other members of the Royal Family. Almost 200,000 people and 25,000 cars had converged on Hendon by the start of the main events, which began promptly at 1500hrs. Some 600 aircraft took part in the flying display on Saturday 26 June, 1937. It was the largest mass formation ever seen in the country up to that time; 250 aircraft consisting of Harrows, Hinds, Gauntlets, Gladiators and Ansons flew over the Royal Enclosure at the start of the programme. This was followed by the regular mix of individual and formation aerobatic demonstrations by Furies, Gauntlets and Gladiators; dog-fights between an Overstrand and No 604 Squadron Demons, Virginias, which had appeared in every display since 1925, and Gladiators; inverted flying by Magisters and comedy routines by a Hart trainer and a WW1 Farman F40 and Monospar SD25 duo. A popular event was an attack on a WW1 observation balloon, defended by a German LVG, by a Sopwith Triplane, a Bristol Fighter and an SE5A. In contrast to these veterans of an earlier conflict, the new and experimental types seen in the air for the first time were the DH93 Don, Miles M9 Kestrel, Airspeed Oxford and Queen Wasp, Blackburn Skua, Fairey P4/34 and Hawker Henley. One of the few civil types on static display was the DH Albatross airliner.

The 1937 display was noteworthy not only for the scale of the flying display, but for the increasing number of camouflaged monoplane bombers that were then entering squadron service, all keenly observed by representatives of several European governments. It was rather ironical that the final event of the display, the traditional set piece, was a small port defended by anti-aircraft guns, barrage balloons, and fighters consisting of Gladiators of No 3 Squadron and Demons of No 601 Squadron which were hard put to keep up with the attacking force of Whitleys of No 10 Squadron, Wellesleys of No 76

A close 'vic' formation of 600 Squadron Hawker Hart I light bombers. The type was replaced by a Hart development, the Demon, in February 1937.

Squadron and Blenheims of No 114 Squadron. And so the exciting and dramatic destruction of the Port Hendon set piece brought the 1937 display to spectacular climax.

Almost as soon as the various participating squadrons had returned to their respective bases they were involved in a series of major training exercises and included amongst the 398 aircraft engaged in a mock attack on London in August, were those belonging to the Hendon-based AAF squadrons. Despite the increasing seriousness of their role, the Auxiliary Squadrons managed to maintain their deceptively casual outlook that continued to attract many memorable personalities from all walks of life. Sqn Ldr Peter Stewart had been replaced by Lord Carlow as Commanding

Officer of No 600 Squadron and fellow peer, the Rt Hon Lord Lloyd of Dolobran, PC, GCSI, DSO, took over as Honorary Air Commodore of the squadron in August.

Within the ranks of No 601 Squadron at this time, known within the squadron as 'The Legion', were several university blues and half a dozen sportsmen of international repute. Michael Peacock, a barrister and widely recognised as the squadron's best aerobatic pilot, had captained Brasenose College Rugby Team at Oxford, skied for Britain as did the flamboyant Roger Bushell, a fellow barrister, while the sports writer and Kent cricketer Aidan Crawley had narrowly escaped death when his Demon crashed earlier in the year. He was rescued from his burning aircraft by his observer, Guy Branch, after crashing on take-off from Netheravon in bad weather during a cross-country flight from Hendon.

Other prominent 'Legionaires' were William H. Rhodes-Moorhouse, son of the early Hendon pioneer and first air VC winner, the Hon J.W. Maxwell Aitken, son of the press baron, Lord Beaverbrook, and Sir Archibald Hope of Craighall, Bt. During the summer of 1937, No 601 Squadron took part in a fictional film about the RAF directed by the Hollywood director, Elmer C. Dyer, who was made an honorary member of the Legion. One fine evening, 'Archie' Hope, who typified the easy-going spirit of the squadron, and a number of 601 pilots took Dyer to Trent Park, another of their Honorary Air Commodore's fine houses, to meet Sir Philip Sassoon. On being asked what he would like to drink, Dyer replied that he understood Sir Philip had some very fine port and he would appreciate a chance to sample it. Sir Philip sent his butler to fetch a bottle of the best port from the cellar. The butler duly brought the bottle covered in cobwebs and the cork was solemnly drawn. The butler poured out a glass for Dyer who raised it to his lips and commented to Sir Philip — 'excellent, quite superb'. He then tipped the rest of his port into his glass of iced coffee. 'Archie' Hope reported that 'Philip stood it very well'.

The more subdued, but no less able pilots of the 'Brains Trust' — No 604 Squadron, included Rory Chisholm, an oil technician and contemporary of Fogarty and Dore, and John Cunningham, a de Havilland test pilot, a relative newcomer who had teamed up with an observer, Jimmy Rawnsley, an electrical engineer by profession. Such was the quality of its aircrews that the squadron was able to win the Lord Esher Trophy for the second and third times in 1936 and 1937.

During the latter half of the year No 24 Squadron began receiving new aircraft types almost weekly. In July, a Miles Nighthawk L6846 was delivered followed a few weeks later by Miles Magister L5931 and on 9 October the squadron received DH86B L7596, a ten-seat biplane powered by four Gipsy Six engines, for use in conveyance of Members of the

Cabinet and Air Council. A second DH86B, G-AENR, was loaned to the squadron by the manufacturer for a short period. In November an additional flight, 'D' Flight, was formed with its aircraft allotted for use by personnel of the Superintendent of Reserve and Inspector of Civil Flying Training Schools. The interim phase of the Royal Air Force's expansion programme between December 1935 and December 1937 had been covered by the Hawker Fury and Hart derivatives,

Gloster Gauntlets and Gladiators and diverse transport, training and communications types, in preparation for the new generation of warplanes such as the Battle, Blenheim, Whitley, Hampden and Wellington bombers, the Lysander army co-operation and Anson and Magister training aircraft. But the most important of the new types were the Spitfire and Hurricane fighters. By January 1938 Fighter Command possessed or was in the process of forming twenty-six Regular and

No 24 Squadron took delivery of this DH86A, modified to B model specification with vertical fins fitted to the tailplane, at the end of 1937.

Auxiliary fighter squadrons, only one of which had taken delivery of its first Hurricanes.

No 111 (F) Squadron, based at Northolt, under the command of 601 Squadron's charismatic ex-Adjutant, Sqn Ldr John Gillan, had replaced one flight of Gauntlets with the new fighter by January. On 10 February, Gillan brought Fighter Command's potent new equipment to the public's attention by flying from Edinburgh to Northolt in a Hurricane, a distance of 327 miles, in only forty-eight minutes; an average speed of 408.75mph. Less newsworthy perhaps, but no less remarkable, was the solo flight in one of No 600's Demons at Hendon in April by fifty-nine-year-old Lord Lloyd, the squadron's Honorary Air Commodore. The following month, Captain Harold Balfour, who had learned to fly at Hendon twenty-three years earlier, was appointed Under-Secretary of State for Air.

The Hurricane was again in the news when No 111 Squadron aircraft made appearances at several of the fifty-eight RAF airfields, including Hendon, that were opened to the public on the fifth Empire Air Day on 28 May. Also seen over Hendon on that day were a trio of tied-together Gladiators from No 87 Squadron and Flt Lt Roger Bushell, who had written-off Max Aitken's private Aeronca G-ADZZ a few days earlier, flying solo aerobatics in a 601 Squadron Demon. The Air Ministry announced earlier in the year that the Royal Air Force display at Hendon was to be discontinued

due to the fact that 'the increasing speed of Service aircraft makes evolutions in a restricted space difficult. Hendon Aerodrome, moreover, is too small for the operations, including the take-off and landing, of large numbers of the higher-powered aircraft now in use'. It was the end of an era.

The tempo of training increased throughout the summer culminating with a total of 945 RAF aircraft taking part in an exercise on 23 August between 'Westland' and 'Eastland', an imaginary territory in the North Sea, whose bombing attacks were met by a fighter defence that included the Auxiliary Air Force Demons, Hurricanes and for the first time, the new Spitfire. On the 25 August Capt H.H. Balfour flew a Spitfire at Duxford, within days of flying a Hurricane which he considered was 'a nice aeroplane for an old gentleman to fly'. The next day all RAF leave was cancelled and Fighter Command brought to an operational state of readiness. The Munich crisis had begun. During this period, Hendon's AAF Squadrons moved to their war stations; 600 Squadron to Kenley, 601 to Biggin Hill and 604 to North Weald, with some of their Demons wearing unfamiliar drab camouflage.

No 24 Squadron continued to operate from Hendon and as the crisis eased, the DH86B left for Khartoum and Nairobi carrying Capt Balfour, the same aircraft had been used earlier in the year to take the Secretary of State for war on an extensive tour of France and Italy. New types continued to be issued, including five DH93 Don communication aircraft which were added to the squadron strength which stood at five Harts, two Audax, one Dragon Rapide, one Nighthawk, one Magister, twenty Miles Mentors and the DH86B on 1 October.

Prime Minister Neville Chamberlain returned from Germany on 30 September having signed the Munich Agreement which allowed Hitler to seize the Czechoslovak frontier region of Sudetenland, Germany having already annexed Austria in March. The Agreement temporarily held Europe back from the brink of all-out war, nevertheless the crisis had given added impetus to the Royal Air Force and Auxiliary Air Force expansion programmes.

Having returned to Hendon, No 601 Squadron began replacing its Demons with Gloster Gauntlets on 31 October and early in January 1939 Nos 600 and 604 Squadrons received their first Blenheim 1Fs having each received an Airspeed Oxford twin-engine trainer apiece. The contrast between the single-engine open-cockpit biplane Demon and the twin-engine enclosed cockpit monoplane Blenheim was considerable and accidents during the intensive training period in the spring were inevitable. On 26 February, Flt Lt Clarke wrote-off L1402, and part of the King's Hangar, and Flg Off Hayes crashed L1398 on take-off on 3 April. Both crews, belonging to 600 Squadron, suffered only

minor injuries. By the end of March, No 601 Squadron had replaced its stop-gap Gauntlets with the Blenheim and at the same time the squadron gained a new recruit — Plt Off Willard Whitney Straight. A very wealthy naturalised American, Whitney Straight had made his name as a racing driver having won the 1935 South African Grand Prix in a Maserati and then turned down an offer to join the all-conquering German Auto Union team as a works driver. He had also entered the 1934 King's Cup air race and commissioned the Miles and Parnall aircraft companies to build two touring aircraft to his specifications. The Miles Whitney Straight was developed into the Monarch which in turn spawned the Nighthawk and Mentor — both of which were serving as high speed communications aircraft with No 24 Squadron at Hendon at the time he joined 601 Squadron. His other two/three-seat design built by Parnall, with the unlikely name of the Hendy Heck IIc, also served in small numbers with 24 Squadron in 1939.

In April, it was announced that a VIP version of de Havilland's new twelve-to-twenty-seat medium-range airliner, the DH95 Flamingo, was ordered for the King's Flight with two more for the use of Air Council Members to be operated by No 24 Squadron.

The 1939 Empire Air Day, held on 20 May, attracted record crowds. In the air and on the ground, drab camouflage predominated. The

ABOVE: The Duke of York, the future King George VI, and the Duchess of York, the present Queen Mother, board a DH86 at Hendon for their first flight together to Brussels on 1 July 1935.

ABOVE RIGHT: The Prince of Wales, on the left, inspecting his new DH60 Gypsy Moth G-AALG which was based at Hendon in the early 1930s. It was later sold to Jean Batten.

RIGHT: A visiting Handley Page Harrow from 37 Sqn at Feltwell misjudged Hendon's runway length on 15 September 1938 ending up just short of the railway lines. Although the aircraft was a write-off there were no serious injuries.

colourful triangles that adorned Hendon's AAF squadrons silver-doped biplanes for nearly a decade had given way to dull code letters painted on 'sand and spinach' camouflage schemes; No 24 Squadron's aircraft being some of the few to retain their pre-Munich silver overall finish.

Another link with Hendon's more colourful past was broken by the untimely death of Sir Philip Sassoon on 2 June. A tireless supporter of British military aviation for more than thirty years, Sir Philip — twice Under-Secretary of State for Air, Commanding Officer and later, Honorary Air Commodore of No 601 Squadron — died at the early age of fifty years, like other Hendon pioneers before him including John Porte and Ned Grosvenor, from a combination of overwork and poor health.

Three weeks later Britain came close to losing its current Air Minister, Sir Kingsley Wood, in an air crash. On 28 June a No 24 Squadron DH86B L7596 crash landed at Kirkby-in-Furness in bad weather while en route from Hendon to Belfast. Although the aircraft was badly damaged, neither the pilot, Wg Cdr D.F. Anderson, nor the passengers, who apart from Sir Kingsley Wood

included Air Marshal Sir Christopher Courtney and Air Vice-Marshal Sholto Douglas, were seriously injured. This accident could have had far-reaching consequences for Britain's defence as war clouds gathered over Europe had any of its illustrious passengers been lost. It also showed up the limitations of carrying VIPs in outdated aircraft fitted only with rudimentary navaids. In consequence, an armed Lockheed Hudson, N7263, was delivered to the King's Flight prior to the arrival of the Flamingo, at Hendon on 4 August, one of the first service aircraft to be purchased from the United States by the Air Ministry.

Large scale exercises in which 1,300 aircraft and 53,000 personnel participated were held over several days in August and by the end of the month the Royal Air Force and RAF reservists were mobilized.

Earlier in the year Neville Chamberlain had finally accepted that Germany's territorial ambitions could no longer be tolerated and had, with France, issued guarantees of protection to Poland. On 1 September Hitler's forces invaded Poland and the following day Britain declared war on Germany.

5 HENDON'S SECOND WORLD WAR

VIPS AND V1S

Following Great Britain's declaration of war on Germany, Hendon's three Auxiliary Air Force squadrons moved to their respective war stations; No 600 (City of London) Squadron to Northolt, No 601 (County of London) Squadron to Biggin Hill and No 604 (County of Middlesex) Squadron to North Weald. Plt Off John Isaacs of 600 Squadron became one of the war's first casualties on 3 September when his Blenheim I crashed in Heading Street, Hendon while practising single-engine approaches to RAF Hendon. This unfortunate accident, which also killed one person on the ground, resulted in the banning of all training flights at Hendon.

Meanwhile, it had been decided that the King's Flight should also be transferred from Hendon, which was both busy and vulnerable, to be rehoused outside the London area. After a number of proposals had been rejected, including Smith's Lawn in Windsor Great Park, the Flight was moved to RAF Benson by the end of September. The King's Flight had been the responsibility of 24 Squadron which found its workload considerably increased as soon as war was declared. Its quarters were moved to those vacated by 604 Squadron on the opposite side

of the station in order to allow for anticipated expansion. Various aircraft were immediately affiliated to the unit including two DH89A Dragon Rapides from Isle of Man Air Services and a Lockheed 10A Electra from British Airways. The Electra, G-AEPR, was used to fly the Prime Minister, Neville Chamberlain, to and from Abbeville in France on 12 September.

From the commencement of hostilities, administrative and flying control of 24 Squadron, under the command of Wg Cdr H.K. Goode, was vested in Fighter Command, and control of the newly-created Air Despatch Letter Service was exercised by the Director of Signals with all other communications purposes controlled by the Director of Staff Duties. Aircraft of 'A' and 'B' Flights were pooled while 'C' Flight was commissioned to carry out the newly-created Air Despatch Letter Service (ADLS) to Amiens and to convey VIPs. Mail was also flown between Hendon and Le Bourget, and VIPs of all ranks, political and military, were flown within the British Isles. A twice daily scheduled service between Hendon and Harrogate was inaugurated on 11 October using Rapides. The Squadron's first DH95 Flamingo was delivered on 21

Hurricane I P3774 was one of twelve 504 Sqn aircraft involved in the interception and downing of five German bombers during a raid on London, during which Buckingham Palace was hit, on 15 September 1940.

King George VI and Queen Elizabeth with the Mayor of Hendon, inspecting the damage following the air raid on Colindale Station on 25 September 1940.

October and by the end of the month the aircraft strength was comprised of two Flamingoes, four Electras, one DH86B, seven Rapides, three Percival Q6s, seven Vega Gulls and one Magister.

On 30 October a new Blenheim squadron, No 248, and a Blenheim conversion unit, was formed at Hendon. Once again it did not take long to discover that Hendon was not the ideal site for multi-engine training and the CU was closed by the end of January 1940 while 248 Squadron moved to North Coates a month later. During the exceptionally cold winter, life at Hendon reverted back to prewar days and there was little activity on the airfield. Groups of Volunteer Reservists and WAAFs arrived unannounced before proper accommodation or duties could be found for them. They were kept occupied with menial tasks while postings to other units were sorted out. The illusion of peacetime routine, however, soon faded as the fighting in Norway intensified.

Winston Churchill, having been appointed First Lord of the Admiralty at the declaration of war, was flown to Le Bourget in one of 24 Squadron's Flamingoes, G-AFUF, on 12 March and during the following two months numerous government ministers, including Chamberlain, made several flights from Hendon to France and Belgium in desperate attempts to stem the German advances. During this period additional aircraft belonging to British Overseas Airways Corporation, formed by

LEFT: One of the few aircraft that remained at RAF Hendon from the first to the last day of World War Two was this USAAF Beechcraft YC-43, 39-139, used by staff of the US Embassy in London. It was later transferred to 24 Squadron.

LEFT: DH95 Flamingo R2765 at Hendon, the second of three pre-war commercial airliners impressed for 24 Squadron soon after the outbreak of war. The aptly named *Lady of Hendon* was regularly used by Winston Churchill before the fall of France.

the merger of Imperial Airways and British Airways on 24 November 1939, were impressed into service with 24 Squadron. Three more Electras and two AW Ensigns were assigned to the recently established 'E' Flight. On 25 April Ensign G-ADST piloted by Flt Lt H.B. 'John' Collins left Hendon for Evanton to pick up a load of ammunition destined for Norway. In the event, Collins was diverted to Lossiemouth to pick up thirty-seven servicemen and their kit and fly them to Wattisham. Within days the defeat of the British Expeditionary Force to Norway was announced.

On the day Germany invaded the Low Countries, 10 May 1940, Neville Chamberlain resigned as Prime Minister in favour of Winston Churchill. With Churchill came a new team of senior ministers including Sir Archibald Sinclair as Secretary of State for Air and Lord Beaverbrook in charge of the newly-created Ministry of Aircraft Production. Both would become familiar figures at Hendon during the war years. Two days later, RAF Spitfires covered a British destroyer crossing the Channel bearing Queen Wilhelmina of the Netherlands, Princess Juliana, Prince Bernhard and their families. Holland had capitulated. Soon after taking office Churchill embarked on a series of flying visits to France in an effort to prevent another defeat at the hands of Germany.

16 May was a crucial day for the British Expeditionary Force (BEF) and Hendon. On that day No 257 Squadron was formed at Hendon with Spitfire 1s and Churchill flew to Le Bourget in 24 Squadron Flamingo AS981 escorted by Spitfires of 92 Squadron to inform the French Government that Britain could spare no more fighters for the defence of France. At the same time some of the heaviest air fighting of the campaign was taking place in the Arras and Amiens sectors which resulted in considerable losses on both sides. The Advance Air Striking Force (AASF) attached to the BEF claimed to have shot down at least forty-five German aircraft while the Luftwaffe caused heavy allied losses both in the air and on the ground. One of the day's casualties was 24 Squadron Dominie (military Rapide) P1764 that was destroyed during an air raid on the British Air Component headquarters at Coulommiers. By the time Churchill returned to Hendon later the same day it was clear that France was on the verge of defeat and that the BEF would have to retreat across the Channel, if possible.

In an effort to bolster the RAF's inadequate transport capability more civil airliners were impressed into service with 24 Squadron including a number of Sabena Savoia-Marchetti SM73s, two of which were promptly destroyed in France on 23 May. One was shot down near Calais and a second damaged on the ground at Merville. Forty-nine-year-old Plt Off Louis Strange, who learned to fly at Hendon in 1913, had rejoined the RAF after an

117

absence of twenty years. He was assigned to lead a flight of 24 Squadron aircraft to Merville carrying mechanics to service damaged RAF aircraft grounded on the airfield. When his own aircraft was destroyed in the bombing, Strange returned to England in a repaired Hurricane, a type he had never flown before. In a time of much confusion and intense activity at Hendon, a detachment of 271 Squadron was formed on 29 May with a varied selection of impressed civil airliners including ex-Imperial Airways' flagship, the HP42 Horsa, an HP Harrow and a Ford Tri-Motor.

The evacuation of the entire BEF from the French port of Dunkirk had begun on May 26 and on the 31st, Churchill made another flight to Paris. On this occasion his Flamingo was escorted from Hendon to Villacoublay by a flight of nine Hurricanes belonging to No 601 Squadron led by Flt Lt 'Archie' Hope who was thanked personally by Churchill before returning home from France. By 5 June, a total of 338,226 Allied troops had been successfully evacuated from Dunkirk by the Royal Navy and a fleet of merchant ships and private craft. Fighter Command flew 2,739 sorties during the evacuation but lost seventy-five pilots killed or captured in the process, including Michael Peacock and Roger Bushell, both of 601 Squadron.

However Churchill remained faithful to France until the last moment. He flew to Gien, thirty-five miles south of Orleans, to meet the French Cabinet

on 11 June, the day after Italy had declared war on Great Britain and France. Two days later he was back at Hendon accompanied by Lord Halifax and Lord Beaverbrook for a last-ditch effort to prevent the fall of France. They flew to Tours where Churchill met the French Prime Minister Paul Reynaud for the last time. The pilot of both these flights in the 24 Squadron Flamingo, undertaken over enemy territory without a fighter escort, was Flt Lt H.B. 'John' Collins who had recently been awarded the DFC for flying ammunition to the BEF in one 24 Squadron's Ensigns. On the same day a 24 Squadron Rapide, one of the last RAF transport aircraft to leave France, flew out of Châteaudun with the remnants of AASF who had had to burn their Hurricanes to prevent them falling into enemy hands. Amongst them was Flg Off Paul Richey of No 1 Squadron who had been fighting in France since the previous October.

This former British Airways Lockheed 10A Electra, ex-G-AEPO, was one of the first American commercial aircraft to be impressed for 24 Squadron at Hendon in 1940.

However, Churchill's missions failed to delay the inevitable and on 22 June France offered the Germans an armistice. There followed a brief period of respite while Britain braced herself for a German onslaught. On 4 July, 257 Squadron, now a Hurricane unit, moved to Northolt and on 27 July, the Princess Royal was able to visit Hendon to present 24 Squadron with two Airspeed Oxford ambulance aircraft, each costing £7,500, donated by the Girl Guides Association which had raised over £50,000 during Guide's Gift Week in May. Two impressed civil Rapide ambulances, Z7258 and Z7261, were also presented to the Squadron by the 'Women of the Empire' and the 'Women of Britain' respectively during another fund raising period — Empire Week.

Another member of the Royal Family to visit the Station was the Duke of Kent who made no less than fourteen flights in and out of Hendon in the

King's Flight Hudson L7263 during the first year of the war. The Duke had almost exclusive use of this aircraft and preferred to use Hendon which was more convenient than the Flight's base at Benson when travelling from London. 24 Squadron's DH86B N6246 was put at the disposal of Lord Trenchard, once again in RAF uniform, for touring the country on morale boosting visits to various air force units and stations.

By August, the frequency of heavy German raids on Channel convoys, coastal installations and fighter airfields in southern England was mounting. The Battle of Britain had begun in earnest. One of the first enemy aircraft to be brought down by defending Spitfires was a Messerschmitt Me-110 which belly-landed in a field near Hawkinge, Kent, and was subsequently displayed at Hendon as part of the town's 'Buy a Spitfire Fund'. As the tempo of the Battle increased, so did flights to and from Hendon by senior RAF officers due to the proximity of the headquarters of Fighter Command at Bentley Priory and No 11 Fighter Group at Uxbridge. Some flew themselves using their unit's aircraft while others had one of 24 Squadron's aircraft assigned to their respective Command.

Bombing raids on Britain increased during August, with airfields ringing London bearing the brunt of daylight raids. On the night of 24 August, the first bombs fell on the City of London and by the end of the month, Fighter Command were flying more than

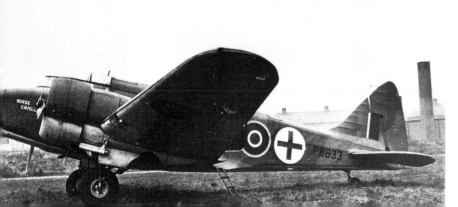

One of two air ambulance Oxford IIs presented to 24 Squadron by the Princess Royal on behalf of the Girl Guides on 27 July 1940. P8833 named *Nurse Cavell* is seen here at Hendon.

1,000 sorties a day, but losses were steadily mounting. Between 24 August and 6 September, 466 RAF fighters were destroyed.

In the early morning of 5 September the outskirts of Hendon were bombed, resulting in the destruction of Messrs Everett & Edgecumbe's factory amongst others. On the same day Hurricanes of No 504 (County of Nottingham) Squadron, veterans of the Battle of France, were transferred to Hendon from Catterick with two Bristol Bombays carrying its heavy equipment. Two days later they were in action against enemy aircraft attacking London from the East. Interception was made over the Thames Estuary towards Margate and in the ensuing combat two German bombers were shot down and another seriously damaged.

Plt Off K.V. Wendel was killed in the engagement while Sgt B.M. Bush made a forced-landing at Eastchurch in his damaged Hurricane. A cannon shell had shattered the windscreen without injuring the pilot. As the Squadron continued to maintain defensive patrols over the capital, Plt Off A.W. Clarke was shot down and killed on 11 September and another Hurricane was damaged beyond repair when its undercarriage collapsed on take-off from Hendon. On the same day a detachment of 59 Squadron with four Blenheim 1Fs arrived at the airfield but stayed only a few days.

Following two days of relative inactivity, the Squadron was brought to readiness at 1100hrs as a party of US Generals and an Admiral arrived at the airfield to see something of the life of an operational RAF fighter squadron. At 1123hrs, just as the pilots were being introduced to their distinguished visitors, the Squadron was scrambled. Twelve Hurricanes took-off in an impressive 4 min 50 sec scramble with orders to rendezvous with 250 Squadron over North Weald at 15,000 ft. At about 1210hrs, the Hurricanes intercepted a formation of Dornier Do 17s at 20,000 ft over southeast London. In the ensuing battle the squadron claimed to have shot down five enemy bombers. One of the Dorniers had been attacking Buckingham Palace when it was brought down by Sgt R.T. Holmes in his first aerial combat. During the chase Holmes' Hurricane P2725 collided with the stricken bomber which crashed in Victoria Station Yard, while Holmes was forced to bale out over Chelsea, landing on a rooftop before sliding down into a neighbouring garden without serious injury. The engagement was witnessed by Queen Wilhelmina from her London home. The Queen of the Netherlands sent a message to Sir Archibald Sinclair congratulating the squadron concerned and the pilot who shot down the German aircraft. However, two other pilots failed to return from the morning's action and it was subsequently confirmed that one of them, Plt Off J.V. Gurteen, had been shot down and killed near Hartley in Kent. Soon after the last Hurricane had returned to Hendon the squadron was again in

A 504 Squadron pilot is helped into his parachute by his ground crew before climbing into his Hurricane I. In only three weeks at Hendon, 504 Squadron claimed seven enemy aircraft and one probable, for the loss of five of its pilots.

action against more raiders between South London and Hornchurch during which another three enemy bombers were claimed for the loss of Flg Off M. Jebb who died from his wounds after baling out over Kent.

During the next ten days 504 Squadron was scrambled on seven occasions without sighting the enemy although a new pilot, Sgt Helcke, was killed when he lost control in a spin during a practice dog-fight on 17 September. Another casualty was visiting Blenheim IV L4906 of 25 Squadron which was written-off, without injuries to the crew, when it overshot on landing at Hendon on the 21st.

Having to fly almost continuous patrols during the day and contend with AA barrages put up against raids over London at night, the pilots had little chance of proper rest in their wooden huts although some of the archways under the railway were converted to blast-proof shelters. At 2015hrs on the 23rd Hendon experienced its first station alarm during which an unexploded shell hit SHQ causing only slight damage. The following night a number of incendiary bombs fell on the airfield and 24 Squadron's hangar, but the fire was quickly extinguished. In the early hours of 25 September, however, a landmine fell on Colindale underground station and surrounding buildings near the airfield perimeter. Fifteen people were killed and many more injured in the raid, including a number of airmen in a train that was entering the station at the time of the explosion. Many of their colleagues spent the rest of the night attempting to reach those trapped in the debris. For many it was their first sight of a dead body. After a brief but hectic period of operations, 504 Squadron moved out to Filton near Bristol on 26 September bringing Hendon's participation in the Battle of Britain to an end.

With the immediate threat of a German invasion now receding the Luftwaffe's Blitz on London reached its height between September and November. On the night of 7 September, 24 Squadron's hangar was destroyed by an oil bomb with the loss of some fourteen aircraft including two Mentors L4396 and L4400, Percival Q6 P5635, Envoy X9370, an Electra, a Blackburn Roc and Air Chief-Marshal Portal's private Vega Gull G-AFIE. A month later several bombs fell on East Camp, the runway and playing fields in West Camp destroying the Maintenance Flight hangar and one aircraft. Two other aircraft were damaged in the raid but no one was injured. No 24 Squadron suffered a further loss when Flamingo R2510 crashed at Mill Hill killing all on board soon after taking-off for Belfast on 23 October. To replace some of the aircraft lost in recent weeks, 24 Squadron took delivery of three Wellington IC transports, with painted turrets and wooden guns, and named the 'Dukes of Cornwall & Rutland'. On 12 November another new unit, No 1 Camouflage Flight, arrived at Hendon. Equipped with an assortment of types, an Oxford, a Lysander and an impressed Leopard Moth, the Flight was responsible for checking the efficiency of concealment of airfields, AA batteries, and munitions factories etc from the air. The Duke of Kent paid the Station an official visit on 10 December by which time Hendon was again settling into a less offensive role, although it remained a target for sporadic bombing raids well into the spring of 1941. On 5 February Sunny Gardens Road close to the airfield and the former home of several early aviation pioneers such as Richard Gates and Reginald Carr, was bombed and several houses destroyed.

More than 200 people had been killed and nearly 1,000 injured by German air raids on the Borough of Hendon during the Blitz. Some 9,000 houses were damaged in the attacks, many of which had been directed at the airfield. In spite of their losses, the local community responded generously to their local 'Four Spitfires Fund' and the 'Cinemas of Britain Spitfire Fund', the latter sponsored by the Gaumont-British Picture Corporation. Hendon collected enough money to buy four Spitfire VBs, subsequently named *Hendon Griffon*, *Hendon Pegasus*, *Hendon Endeavour* and *Hendon Lamb* while each cinema in the area raised money towards three Spitfire IIs known collectively as the 'Gaumont-British Flight'.

Various other units formed at Hendon in the spring of 1941 including No 1416 (Recce) Flight

with Spitfire IIs and Blenheim IVs on 10 March and No 1 Delivery Flight two weeks later. No 116 (Calibration) Squadron, the RAF's first specialist flight equipped with Lysanders, Oxfords, Puss Moths and Hurricane Is, arrived from Hatfield in April. This unit flew calibration sorties for the Observer Corps, anti-aircraft guns and searchlights. Inevitably there were a number of accidents during this period, although none were due to enemy action or caused serious injuries. In April, No 1 Camouflage Unit, formally Flight, lost one of its Dominies when R9551 crashed away from base following an engine failure, and yet another visiting Blenheim IV, T1825 of 105 Squadron flown by Plt Off H.I. Edwards, crashed on landing at Hendon on 20 May.

While several non-flying units such as a Re-fuelling and Re-arming Party and an Anti-Aircraft Flight were also formed during 1941, the major operator remained 24 Squadron. With some 50 aircraft on strength by mid-1941 the squadron flew a network of VIP, ambulance and scheduled general service flights within Britain and Northern Ireland. No 24 was unlike any other RAF operational squadron. Many of the crews had been civil airline pilots before the war, from a number of different countries. The majority managed to acquire sleeping-out passes and at 1700 hrs there tended to be a general exodus. At the same time there was the possibility of being detached at short notice for long periods away from Hendon, only returning when

Hendon Lamb was one of four Spitfire Vs, the others were W3332 *Hendon Griffon*, W3333 *Hendon Pegasus*, and W3505 *Hendon Endeavour*, presented by the Hendon residents. *Hendon Lamb*, Spitfire V W3506 was lost on 12 April 1942 when serving with 303 Squadron.

their aircraft required maintenance. These circumstances somewhat thwarted the Air Ministry's attempt to encourage a close squadron social life.

To this end, a YMCA canteen, managed by Rupert Bruce-Lockhart and his wife, was opened during the height of the Battle of Britain. The well-appointed canteen, the first on an operational RAF station at the time, was situated below the control tower, which dated back to the Grahame-White era, and included a Quiet Room and a small theatre. Through their extensive theatrical connections, Bruce-Lockhart and his wife were able to persuade many well-known stars of the day to appear on the Hendon stage, including Dorothy Dickson, Beatrice Lillie, Edith Evans and Bernard Miles, to entertain the airmen. Some of the acts proved to be of a rather sophisticated nature and not always appreciated by the audience. Many of the airmen preferred the more down-to-earth entertainment to be found in the local pubs. Droves of well-meaning lady volunteers also found their way to Hendon to

help in the canteen but during the frequent air raid alerts, airmen found that the shelters had been taken over by the YMCA ladies.

Although London enjoyed something of a respite in the summer of 1941, the Allies suffered a series of defeats in Greece, Yugoslavia, Crete and Libya and Britain was struggling to maintain its vital Atlantic lifeline. The situation was only marginally eased at the end of June when Hitler launched 'Operation Barbarossa', Germany's invasion of its erstwhile ally, Russia. In the meantime the RAF was left virtually free to build the nucleus of an attacking force with the introduction of a new generation of multi-engined long-range bombers and the frantic movement of units from one base to another had settled to an orderly relocation of resources.

On 5 September 1416 Flight moved to Benson, the RAF's photo-reconnaissance centre, to become No 140 Squadron. Two days later one of Hendon's four presentation Spitfire VBs, W3333 *Hendon Pegasus*, was lost in a mid-air collision. Assigned to No 129 Squadron at Westhampnett in Sussex, W3333 was being flown by Sgt P. Boddy in a formation practice when he collided with his leader. Although the leader was able to glide back to base where he landed safely, Boddy was obliged to bale out leaving *Hendon Pegasus* to dive into Chichester Harbour.

By the end of 1941, RAF Hendon had some 123 aircraft on strength, almost half belonging to 24 Squadron which lost one of them on 10 December

A line-up of Wellington ICs, including DG-E of 1665 HCU and EO-Z of 150 TU, at Hendon on 5 September 1941 before departure to Benson to form part of 140 Squadron.

when a Whitney Straight BD145, one of three impressed into the Squadron, crashed en route to the airfield.

Two days previously, the United States of America had entered the War following the Japanese attack on Pearl Harbor and on 22 December, Lord Beaverbrook and Air Chief-Marshal Sir Charles Portal accompanied Winston Churchill to Washington for a conference with President Roosevelt. America's entry in the war accelerated deliveries of US aircraft under the Lend-Lease agreement of March 1941, especially the Lockheed Hudson, six of which were in service with 24 Squadron by the spring of 1942. Another US type to arrive at Hendon was Beech YC-43 39-139 for use by the US Military Air Attaché in London while the US Naval Attaché's Puss Moth was transferred to 'A' flight of 24 Squadron.

Coinciding with a marked increase in the Atlantic ferry of US types, Hendon was transferred to Ferry Command on 1 April with 24 Squadron. Prestwick and Portreath, entry points for ferry flights, were added to the constantly expanding route network. The early months of 1941, however, proved to be a period of triumph and tragedy for the Squadron.

On 20 April No 116 (Calibration) Squadron left Hendon to take up residence at Heston and the following day three 24 Squadron aircraft, Hudson AM725, Dominie X7374 and DH86B N6246, were destroyed in an accidental hangar fire. The

spectacular fire was witnessed by Sir Stafford and Lady Cripps as they landed at Hendon on the last leg of a journey from India. Sir Stafford Cripps thanked his reception party for putting on such a good display on his arrival. A week later, one of the Squadron's impressed Stinson Reliants, W7978, crashed in an adjacent field having suffered an engine failure on take-off from Hendon. Although no one was seriously hurt on this occasion, a very much more serious incident occurred the following month.

During visits to Washington and London to pressure the Western Allies into opening up a second front in Europe as soon as possible, Russia's Foreign Secretary Viachislav Molotov landed at RAF Teeling near Dundee on 7 May en route for a meeting with Churchill at Chequers. That morning

One of several Wellington C.XVIs that were operated by 24 Squadron in the early 1940s. The type had the front and rear turrets removed, the bomb-bay sealed, and seats installed in the fuselage.

a 24 Squadron Flamingo was despatched to Scotland to pick up members of the Russian delegation. However, on the return flight to Hendon the Flamingo caught fire in the air and crashed in the Vale of York killing all those on board including several members of Molotov's staff, senior RAF personnel and the pilot, Flg Off Ramsey. The Russians immediately claimed that the aircraft had been sabotaged and demanded that the duty NCO in charge of its pre-flight inspection at Hendon, a Corporal A. Dance, be shot. Thankfully this was not carried out and the cause of the accident showed that there was no error by the maintenance crew although the incident did nothing to dispel mutual suspicion between the Allies.

A more rewarding period in the Squadron's history, however, began on 31 May with the inauguration of regular mail and passenger flights to the beleaguered island of Malta using unarmed Lockheed Hudsons. The following day No 1 Camouflage Unit was transferred from Hendon to Stapleford Tawney and a week later No 2722 Squadron of the RAF Regiment arrived to take over the airfield's ground defences, although by this time air raids were thankfully few and far between. Air Ambulance Orderlies, messed at Hendon Hall, began training on the airfield during June.

A further incident involving another 24 Squadron Flamingo also ended tragically, although again through no fault of any of the Squadron personnel

concerned. On 24 August the Squadron received an order from the Air Ministry to prepare a Flamingo for a VIP flight. While ground running the Bristol Perseus engines, an escape hatch broke loose and flew into the propellers. The Flamingo was immediately declared unserviceable by its conscientious ground crew. However, its intended passenger, who as it transpired was the Duke of Kent, had a tight schedule to keep for a visit to RAF units in Iceland so took an overnight train to Scotland. Here the Duke and his party joined a Coastal Command Sunderland of 228 Squadron at the Cromarty base of Invergordon for the flight to Iceland. Within an hour of taking off the flying-boat crashed into high ground in overcast conditions near the village of Berriedale in Caithness. All on board, except the rear gunner, were killed in the accident. A week later it fell to Hendon to provide the bearer party and escort, made up of airmen of No 2722 Squadron, for the Duke of Kent's remains at his funeral.

The size and complexity of 24 Squadron had by mid-1942 grown almost to wing size. Having taken delivery of five Lockheed 12As, two impressed Fokker FXXIIs and a Bristol Bombay, and with almost weekly additions to its tasks at home and abroad, it was decided to form a new squadron from within its ranks. On 15 October 'A' Flight became No 510 Squadron with the new unit taking over a diverse collection of pre-war air-taxis including many impressed civil touring types such as a Puss

Moth and a Gipsy Moth, as well as a vintage Hawker Hart and a Curtiss Mohawk fighter.

Coinciding with the establishment of the new RAF unit, the first United States Navy unit, Fleet Aircraft Service Squadron (FASRON 76), was formed at Hendon equipped with R4D-1s, the USN version of the DC-3. The United States Army Air Force (USAAF) was also more in evidence on the airfield towards the end of the year, with flights bringing senior US military personnel to London for liaison meetings with their British counterparts. On 28 November the pilot of visiting Hurricane P3757 from HQ Squadron Det VIII USAFSC mis-judged his approach to Hendon's short runway and crashed on overshoot, luckily without personal injury. With yet more and larger aircraft moving to Hendon, long overdue work on a new tarmac runway commenced during the autumn and continued throughout the winter months.

No 24 Squadron, now commanded by Wg Cdr H.B. Collins, was the only squadron in the RAF to be given authority to fly at any time and in any weather — often without radio or normal navigation aids, and was entitled by King's Regulations to take-off with or without the station commander's permission. Pilots came from Canada, Australia, France, Belgium, Holland, Czechoslovakia, Poland and the United States as well as Britain. Many were highly experienced ex-airline pilots such as two Dutch flight commanders, Lt Jan Rykhof, a pre-war KLM Captain who was the only pilot that Queen Wilhelmina would fly with — and never above 5,000ft — and Sqn Ldr Blennerhassett. Another ex-KLM captain was the Czech Carl Balik who was joined by his compatriot Joe Hubachek, Czechoslovakia's aerobatic champion. Sous-Lieutenant Perrier had fought in the Battle of France while the Belgian Jacques Carlier, a barrister before the war, had survived a mid-air collision with a Lysander while flying a Spitfire during the Battle of Britain but suffered severe burns. One of the squadron's most respected pilots was Charlie Willis, a Volunteer Reserve pilot whose wife flew with the ATA. Another VR Officer was pre-war matinee idol John Justine who gave up a lucrative Hollywood film contract to fly at Hendon under the name of John de Ledesma.

The Malta Shuttle, however, was a remarkable achievement by the Squadron that was given little or no recognition at the time. It had started when Malta was still being pounded around the clock by the Luftwaffe in order to prevent attacks being mounted from the island on Axis shipping in the Mediterranean as Rommel mounted a new offensive in North Africa. Single Hudsons would fly from Hendon to Portreath in Cornwall loaded with passengers and urgent supplies. The unescorted aircraft would then depart at midnight for a hazardous six-hour flight in darkness to Gibraltar via the Bay of Biscay. Following another midnight take-off the Hudson was often held off Malta during night raids on the island on arrival. Within hours the aircraft was retracing its steps to Hendon carrying battle-weary aircrews at the end of their tour, wounded servicemen and the occasional captured German General. On 4 July 1942 General Hertzberg, who had been captured in the Western desert, was flown from Malta to Hendon for interrogation in England. No 24 Squadron flew a total of 323 shuttle flights and 10,000 flying hours to Malta carrying 5,552 passengers and 70 tons of freight — and the George Cross awarded to the people of the Island for their courage by King George VI. Amongst the passengers were several special agents, using the name 'L.A. Prune', who left the aircraft at Gibraltar to make their way into occupied Europe. Following his success at El Alamein in February 1943 a party of British Generals was flown from Hendon to Tripoli in two Hudsons to meet Montgomery at his headquarters in North Africa. The aircraft then made a quick dash across the Mediterranean to Malta before returning to pick up the Generals and fly them back to Hendon the following day. Only four Hudsons were lost during the Malta shuttle, which was testimony to the high standards of 24 Squadron's air and ground crews operating in extremely difficult conditions.

The squadron's passenger lists were peppered with VIPs from all over the world. King Peter of Yugoslavia, King George of Greece, Emir Faisal of Iraq, Stanislaw Mikolajczyk, Poland's Prime Minister in Exile and General Jan Smuts, South Africa's Prime Minister, were all carried by 24 Squadron between 1942-3. During the same period the Squadron found time to give local Air Training Corps cadets 'flips' in some of the older types such as the Dominie, DH86B and the Fokker XXIIs, although the latter had been transferred to No 1680 Flight in Scotland by October 1942.

More US Douglas C-47s (Dakotas) began arriving at Hendon, designated by the USAAF as Station 575, during April 1943 when the 86th Squadron of the 27th Group VIIIth Air Force Service Command was formed. To supplement the C-47s, three Dominies were transferred from 24 Squadron to the US Group. By the end of the month 24 Squadron received the first of its Dakota Is, FD772 named *Windsor Castle*, and a few days later another new type about to enter service with the squadron made a dramatic landing at Hendon. The first Avro York C(VIP) LV633, a passenger development of the Lancaster bomber, flew into the airfield with Avro's test-pilot Bill Thorn at the controls. The large four-engined transport, destined to become Churchill's personal aircraft and later christened by Wg Cdr Collins *Ascalon*, managed to land on Hendon's notoriously short undulating main runway successfully, albeit with little room to spare. However, after taxying and turning in front of the control tower, one of its huge main-wheels sank into the tarmac up to the hubs. Following a major operation to extricate the York, it was decided that in future the aircraft should be operated from Northolt.

Amongst the service personnel of note flown by the squadron during May was Wg Cdr G. Gibson who was given a priority flight to Manston in a Proctor a few days prior to leading 617 Squadron's famous raid on the Moehne and Eder Dams in Germany. Air Chief-Marshal Tedder was a frequent visitor to the station often arriving unannounced at the controls of his own Proctor. On 31 May, Viscount Trenchard left Hendon at the start of an extensive tour of North Africa and Malta in a 24 Squadron Hudson. During the three week trip, the seventy-one-year-old 'Father of the RAF' made a total of thirty-two landings and take-offs and on his return wrote personally to the crew thanking them for looking after him so well despite the uncomfortable conditions. Other VIPs carried during this period included Lord Louis Mountbatten, Gen Archibald Nye, Vice-Chief of Imperial General Staff, and Free-French leader General Henri Giraud.

While a steady stream of Dakotas were being delivered to Hendon's squadrons, one of the last of the ex-Imperial Airways DH Albatross airliners *Fortuna*, that had been impressed for service with 271 Squadron, took off from Hendon on 16 July with fifteen passengers aboard abound for Shannon.

On approach to its destination the Albatross suffered a structural failure and crashed. Although the aircraft was destroyed in the accident the passengers and crew escaped serious injury.

On 1 August yet another new squadron was formed out of 24 Squadron. No 512 Squadron, equipped with Dakotas took over the flights to Portreath, Prestwick and Gibraltar. By the end of the year the new squadron had lost three Dakotas on these routes, two on take-off from Portreath,

The first Douglas DC-3 Dakota I, FD772 *Windsor Castle*, delivered to 24 Squadron in October 1942, is seen here at Hendon in March 1943.

This pristine Dakota III, KG647, was delivered to the newly-formed 512 Squadron at Hendon in late 1943.

FL515 & FL545, while FD903 crashed in Spain en route for Gibraltar. In October the USAAF began a similar operation. Known as the 'Marble Arch Line', three C-47s (Dakotas) flew scheduled services between Hendon and St Mawgan and Prestwick. Hendon was also the centre for numerous ancillary units such as the Book Production and Distribution Centre which had moved into Aeroville, also the main WAAF accommodation, while the No 2 Casualty Air Evacuation Unit, which was to play an important role in future events, arrived by the end of the year.

With the imminent prospect of an Allied invasion of occupied Europe the tempo of life at Hendon increased appreciably in the New Year. In January 1944, No 116 (Transport Command) Wing, authorised to operate internal air transport and airline services between the United Kingdom and India, established its Headquarters at the Hendon Hall Hotel. A USAAF C-47 Conversion Section was added to Hendon's establishment, and yet another Dakota squadron, No 575, was formed out of 512 Squadron. No 1 Air Despatch and Reception Unit Detachment was formed at Hendon to handle passengers, freight and mail by air. The total handled in January was 203 passengers in and 48 out, with 20,111lb of freight and mail, in and 51,983lb out. On 14 February Nos 512 and 575 Squadrons left Hendon for Broadwell giving valuable breathing space for the remaining units. A

few weeks later the Station acquired a mascot in the form of a donkey that was won in a night-club raffle by members of 510 Squadron. The donkey, named Barnes, was transported from the West End to Hendon by tube train and given the honorary rank of Pilot Officer. On 8 April 510 Squadron ceased to exist when it was re-named the Metropolitan Communications Squadron (MCS). At the time, the MCS had some seventy-five aircraft on establishment including thirty-one Proctors, ten Dominies, seven Hudsons, five Ansons, a Grumman Goose amphibian reserved for the Secretary of State for Air and two Spitfire Is used for refresher flying by senior officers.

Soon after D-Day, the long-awaited Allied invasion of Normandy on 6 June, 24 Squadron Dakotas flew around the clock in support of the 2nd Tactical Air Force (RAF) flying in supplies and returning with wounded tended by the Air Casualty Unit. Sgt Albert Edwards, one of the first volunteer Air Ambulance Orderlies to undergo training at Hendon Hall in 1942, won the AFM during D-Day CASEVACs. While a foothold on the continent was being established, Hendon again found itself a target for German air-raids. On the night of 30 June one wing of Colindale Hospital was hit by a V1 flying-bomb killing four airmen and injuring many others. Part of the WAAF quarters at Aeroville were also damaged by the explosion, seriously injuring a number of them.

In June the prototype of the Miles M28 Messenger U-0223, which was a short take-off single-engine liaison aircraft designed as a possible replacement for MCS's miscellaneous collection of pre-war Miles and DH touring aircraft, was written-off at Hendon. It had been lent to one of the squadron's pilots who struck the corner of a hangar during take-off, destroying the aircraft in the process and having to be rescued — uninjured — from the hangar roof.

A frequent visitor to Hendon, since learning to fly in England in 1942, was Prince Bernhard of the Netherlands who had the exclusive use of firstly impressed Miles Whitney Straight DP237 and later the ex-US Embassy and 24 Squadron Beech D17 Traveler DR628. These aircraft were subsequently replaced by Lockheed 12A NF753 which was part of Dutch Air Force No 1316 Communications Flight established at Hendon on 7 July. Apart from the Royal Lockheed, the flight comprised four Dominies, one Hudson, a Proctor and two Auster IIIs, all ex-MCS aircraft. In the wake of the D-Day landings, the Flight began flying into Europe in support of Dutch units in the British Army.

Meanwhile, on the evening of 27 July an RAF Dakota touched down at Hendon after a flight from North Africa. On board was a member of the Polish resistance clutching parts of a V2 rocket smuggled out of Poland following a dramatic flight into enemy territory by the same Dakota.

Although an Allied victory was now in sight, Germany was determined to fight on to the bitter end as Hendon found out to its cost in August 1944. On the 3rd, just a day after three aircrew had been killed when a 24 Squadron Hudson crashed after taking-off from Hendon, a V1 flying-bomb hit the southeast corner of the airfield killing nine airmen and wounding another twenty-five. Several buildings were badly damaged and five aircraft destroyed. A tragic sequel to the raid occurred two days later when Air Vice-Marshal O.T. Boyd collapsed and died following a heart attack while visiting the injured and inspecting damage at Hendon.

Following the breakout from Normandy by General Patton's 3rd Army, an additional ten USAAF C-47s were added to the strength of the USATC at Hendon to provide additional support to the Allies' push towards the German Border. In September the US unit began regular flights to Versailles for SHAEF personnel — a similar service to that flown by the RAF during the closing months of WW1 a quarter of a century earlier.

The airfield was fortunate to escape further enemy damage when a V2 rocket exploded in the air over Colindale in the first week of October. At the time some 200 aircraft, many of them Dakotas, were on strength with the four home-based squadrons. The MCS had no less than seventy-four aircraft on establishment while 24 Squadron, which had recently standardised on Dakotas and Ansons, possessed another forty. The station's facilities were close to their limits handling such large numbers but the situation was considerably eased when USATC moved its fifty plus C-47s to Bovingdon on 16 October. This did not, however, mean the end of USAAF movements to Hendon. Apart from a steady flow of VIP flights to and from the continent, several battleweary B-17 Fortresses and B-24 Liberators, involved in the round-the-clock raids on Germany, made tyre-bursting emergency landings on the airfield during the following months.

As the war continued unabated into its sixth long year, many of Hendon's aircraft were dispersed at various airfields in the British Isles and Europe. Apart from directly supporting the Allied forces, 24 Squadron flew scheduled airmail and priority passenger flights to Scotland and Northern Ireland. One of the pilots flying VIPs on the Belfast route during the early months of 1945 was Jimmy Edwards, who had won a DFC flying Dakotas during the doomed Arnhem operation. He was also one of a number of squadron pilots who questioned the wearing of 'best blue' uniforms when flying VIPs during wartime. However, 24 Squadron's Dakotas were also used for a number of pioneering experiments using the latest navigation aids, such as Loran and radar altimeters, so paving the way for safer air travel in the future. On the lighter side, trips to such destinations as North Africa, Gibraltar and Portugal enabled aircrews to acquire certain luxury goods — perfumes, spirits, nylon stockings etc — that were not readily available at home, and it was not unusual for the odd package to drop out of the back of a Dak as it taxied round Hendon's peritrack after an overseas flight. Life for the 2,000 officers, airmen, and women, stationed at Hendon, however, began to relax as the fear of enemy raids receded. The Station Theatre again flourished with high quality attractions such as S/Ldr Ralph Reader and his RAF Gang Show regularly topping the bill.

By the middle of March 1945, the Allies were on the German borders and a few of its leaders, recognising the inevitable, began making tentative attempts to arrange an armistice. Heinrich Himmler, Hitler's notorious SS Chief, was one of them. In April Count Folke Bernadotte, the Vice-President of the Swedish Red Cross who had been working in Germany arranging for the repatriation of Danish and Norwegian political prisoners, arrived in London with an offer from Himmler to surrender to the Western Allies on condition that the war against the Soviet Union would continue. On 27 April, Count Bernadotte flew out of Hendon with the Allies rejection of the proposal. Three days later, Hitler committed suicide in his Berlin bunker.

During the last days of the war in Europe, aircraft movements at Hendon increased as a constant flow of high ranking Allied officers, British Members of

An aerial view looking south, of RAF Hendon taken in May 1943, soon after the completion of the new 1,159 yard secondary runway. Note the number of transport type's widely dispersed around the airfield, and the close proximity of suburbia in the foreground. The RAF Museum hangars are to be seen at the top left hand quarter of the airfield.

King George VI, Queen Elizabeth, and Princess Elizabeth arrive at RAF Hendon aboard 24 Sqn Dakota VIP IV KN386 on 19 July 1945 following a visit to Northern Ireland.

Parliament, doctors and Commissions crossed the Channel as Germany was overrun and its notorious concentration camps were discovered. On 3 May an Allied team of scientists and British Technical Intelligence Officers flew from Hendon to Lichtenau on a secret visit to the recently captured V2 test and assembly centre at Nordhausen only hours before the area was occupied by Soviet troops.

Following the final German surrender on 8 May, Hendon experienced one of the busiest periods in its history. Apart from receiving wounded troops, the resident Air Ambulance unit remained in operation until the end of hostilities, and repatriated Allied PoWs, governments and Heads of State in exile began to return to countries they had not set foot in for more than five years.

In June, Hendon could again lay claim to being the home of the Royal Flight. On 1 June, Dakota IV KN386 of 24 Squadron was selected as the personal transport of King George VI and the Royal Family. The following day, Queen Elizabeth of the Belgians flew into Hendon from Evere to pay her first visit to Britain since being confined in the Palace of Laeken near Brussels since the German occupation of Belgium in May 1940. The Queen left Hendon on 15 June in a 24 Squadron Dakota flown by S/Ldr Jacques Cartier, the Belgian barrister who had escaped across the channel five years earlier to fly Spitfires in the Battle of Britain. On the same day the Danish Royal Family flew home via Lüneberg in another 24 Squadron Dakota piloted by F/Lt G.H. Duncan. On the 23rd, Queen Juliana of the Netherlands made an emotional departure in yet another Dakota, FZ631, accompanied by a squadron of Polish Hurricanes from Northolt. At the end of the month, King George VI accompanied by Queen Elizabeth and Princess Elizabeth arrived from Long Kesh at the end of a visit to Northern Ireland.

Aircraft movements at Hendon during June 1945 totalled 3,858, of which 3,593 were made by the RAF and 265 by the USAAF. As the victorious Allies attempted to come to terms with the chaos of post-war Europe, heavy fighting continued in the Far East as Japan prepared itself for a last ditch defence of its homeland. However, following the dropping of atomic bombs on Hiroshima and Nagasaki, the Japanese signed an instrument of unconditional surrender on board the US battleship *Missouri* in Tokyo Bay on 2 September.

Hendon's second world war had ended.

6 UNDER NOTICE

THE END OF AN ERA

The end of hostilities brought little immediate respite for the transport squadrons based at Hendon. While Europe was in chaos, 24 Squadron continued the role of an embryo airline in support of the occupation forces. In August 1945, one of its Dakota IVs, KN628, with a crew led by the newly-promoted S/Ldr G.H. Duncan, was assigned to the Chief of the Imperial General Staff, Field Marshal Montgomery. The following month the Squadron was selected by Transport Command to begin an air service between Blackbushe and Prestwick to be operated in all weathers and obtain experience of available radio and allied aids to navigation, approach and landing in adverse weather conditions. Two Dakotas and three experienced crews were assigned to the service scheduled to fit in with trans-Atlantic arrivals at Prestwick.

On 15 September, Hendon held a Station 'Open Day' that attracted some 60,000 spectators, many of whom had attended the last great pre-war RAF Display — eight long years earlier. Displayed on the Open Day, apart from the resident RAF and US Navy transport aircraft, were fighters including the Typhoon, Tempest, Mustang and Mosquito, nautical types such as the Barracuda, Walrus, Sea Otter and Warwick, and two 'heavies' in the shape

An early post-war shot of a 24 Squadron Dakota IV at Hendon prominently wearing its serial KN512 in large letters under the wings, and the code AKW on the nose.

ABOVE: 'This accident was entirely due to the gross incompetence of the pilot.' These comments were written in his crash report by the pilot Flt Lt Jeremy Howard-Williams, 604 Sqn's Adjutant after belly-landing his Spitfire LF.XVI RAK-W on 24 August 1947.

BELOW: Former 604 Squadron Spitfire LF.XVI RW382 is still airworthy in 1994.

ABOVE: 'Spotters' outside the main-gate of RAF Hendon in October 1951 with No 142 GS glider in the background. The Guard House on the left survived until 1992.

BELOW: The last US Unit to leave RAF Hendon was the US Army's 32nd Anti-Aircraft Artillery Brigade which arrived in 1954. This is one of its L-20A Beavers.

of a Stirling and Lancaster. The star attraction of this first post-war public display was an RAF Sikorsky R-4 Hoverfly helicopter.

A familiar visitor, as the Prince of Wales, and later King Edward VIII, when Hendon had been the base for the Royal aircraft, was the now Duke of Windsor. He arrived from Le Bourget in a 24 Squadron Dakota, KN624, on 5 October for a short private visit. Six days later the Duke left for France from Hendon, aboard another 24 Squadron Dakota, KJ980, for what was to be his last official flight on an RAF aircraft. Amongst those at the airfield to bid him farewell was his old friend, Air Commodore E.H. Fielden, Captain of the King's Flight. A more tragic incident occurred a month later when an RAF Mustang, flown by Wing Commander Derek Walker, a distinguished wartime fighter leader, commanding officer of the first Meteor squadron and married to Diana Barnato, the equally distinguished ATA pilot, crashed into houses in the circuit at Hendon killing the pilot.

The first full year of peace began with a comprehensive re-organisation of units at Hendon. By the end of 1945, administration of the station had been transferred to 46 Group of Transport Command while the Headquarters of 65 Group of Reserve Command moved to Hendon. At the same time, runways 34/16 and 02/20 were re-surfaced and a number of the station's buildings refurbished.

On 25 February 1946, 24 Squadron moved to Bassingbourn thus bringing to an end thirteen years

The United States Embassy re-established its relationship with Hendon by forming the US Air Attaché Flight using Spitfire PR.XI PL983/NC74138 based at the airfield. The aircraft was successfully flown in a number of air races by the former ATA pilot, Lettice Curtis.

of unbroken operations from the airfield. One of the reasons for transferring 24 Squadron, was the sheer numbers of aircraft that were based at Hendon in the immediate post-war period. The US Navy transport squadron VR-24 detachment with a fleet of navalised Dakotas, R4Ds, continued to support US Sixth Fleet operations in the Mediterranean while the Metropolitan Communications Squadron (MCS) had no less than seventy-seven aircraft on strength in 1946 of more than ten different types, ranging from a Miles Messenger to a Hawker Tempest fighter.

The gap left by 24 Squadron paved the way for re-establishing units of the Auxiliary Air Force at Hendon after a seven year absence. Appropriately enough, the Squadrons chosen to re-form on 10 May were 601 (County of London), under the command of Sqn Ldr Max Aitken, and 604 (County of Middlesex), commanded by Sdr Ldr John Cunningham. Both squadrons were equipped with Harvard trainers and Spitfire LF.16s. It was incongruous that Hendon, which had been deemed unsuitable as a fighter base during the Battle of Britain, should now operate the more powerful marks of Spitfire operated by the two AAF units, the MCS and a PR.XI used for high speed courier duties with the US Air Attaché Flight formed on 27 January 1946. During this period, the Metropolitan Communications Squadron began to shed some of its more obscure types and standardise on Ansons

and Proctors. Many of its aircraft, particularly Dominies and Austers, had been assigned to Allied Chiefs of Staffs in exile, such as Belgium and Holland, and these were now in the process of being transferred to their respective governments.

The strong relationship that Hendon enjoyed with Holland was maintained and in June 1946, Queen Juliana and Prince Bernhard arrived at the airfield in a Royal Netherlands Air Force Dakota, 971, for a short visit to London. The following year another flying unit was formed at Hendon, the B.A.F.O. (UK) Communications Flight equipped with Ansons. Meanwhile, a steady stream of VIPs continued to visit the Station. Field Marshal Montgomery made several flights in MCS Ansons having relinquished his personal Dakota, and on 17 July the Duchess of Kent attended a Junior Air Corps rally and air display at Hendon.

The end of another era took place on 1 September when the last WAAF stationed at Hendon moved out of Aeroville leaving only the Air Ministry Book Production and Distribution Centre to occupy Grahame-White's historic aviation buildings. In the meantime, the Auxiliary Air Force Squadrons were flourishing. Both 601 and 604 Squadrons already had a sizeable waiting list of highly experienced pilots wishing to join. Pre-war traditions were maintained, and Viscount Templewood, formerly Sir Samuel Hoare, resumed office as Honorary Air Commodore of 604 Squadron, and the Squadrons settled down to a familiar routine of weekend flying and summer camps. Despite their pilots' considerable experience, all had to have at least 1,500 flying hours, most of which had been amassed during wartime operations, the occasional mishap was recorded. However, a belly landing by one of 604 Squadron's Spitfires flown by F/Lt Howard-Williams was the most serious accident to befall the post-war AAF flyers. On 16 December 1947, King George VI gave permission for the 'Royal' prefix to be used by the Auxiliary Air Force.

At the beginning of the new year, Hendon was again forcefully reminded of the close proximity of the airfield and those who lived and worked on its boundaries. On 9 February, a Metropolitan

Auxiliary airmen of 604 County of Middlesex Squadron, which re-formed at Hendon on 10 May 1946, servicing Spitfire LF.XVI RW382, in April 1947. This aircraft remains airworthy in 1994.

Flt Lt Howard-Williams in 604 Squadron Spitfire LF.XVI TE439 NG-R at RAF Hendon on 14 September 1947 prior to flying to Heathrow for a Battle of Britain display.

12 Spitfires of 601 County of London Squadron, on the left, and 604 Auxiliary Air Force Squadron lined up at RAF Hendon for their 1947 Annual Inspection. Note VRU-4 Douglas R4D-5, Beechcraft JRB-6, and extremely rare Howard GH-1, transports in the background.

Communications Squadron Anson C.19, TX168, crashed at Burnt Oak Broadway. In an accident that mirrored that of P/Off Isaac's Blenheim nine years earlier, the Anson had been practising single-engine approaches to the airfield when it lost power, clipped several buildings and a trolley-bus, before crashing in flames near a garage. The Anson's pilot, Wing Commander Rolfe, and the co-pilot Fl/Lt MacLeakin, were killed instantly while nine others were injured on the ground. A number of other people, including those on the trolley-bus, had a narrow escape. The cause of the accident was subsequently found to be that the crew had attempted to obtain increased power on the engine being feathered, but had omitted to switch the fuel supply on.

The take-off performance of some heavily laden US Navy R4Ds was also a cause for alarm and in the event of an aircraft failing to become airborne prior to reaching the railway line at the end of the runway, Hendon Air Traffic Controllers had direct control over the railway signals in the area which could be switched to red in an emergency. It was also one of the few RAF airfields where flying had to stop when a Royal train was due past. Another potential hazard to air traffic in the area were two 93ft High Frequency aerials belonging to an RAF Transmitting Station situated in the middle of a sports field at Canons Park, Edgware. The Station was manned by the RAF Signals section stationed at Hendon.

604 Squadron Spitfire LF.XVIs NG-H, foreground, and RAK-T prepared for the weekend's flying in 1948. RAK identification letters were carried by the training flight's Harvards and Spitfires, and NG by the operational flight's Spitfires.

However, in spite of the less than ideal operating conditions, the number of aircraft movements actually increased during this period with flying taking place seven days a week. The flourishing Royal Auxiliary Air Force squadrons flew most weekends and continued to attract ex-wartime flyers from all walks of life. One of the most-respected amongst their number was Sqn/Ldr H.S.L. 'Cocky' Dundas, who took over command of 601 Squadron in June 1948.

On 19 July, the Metropolitan Communications Squadron became 31 Squadron, which had operated in the Middle East and India for the previous thirty-three years. The 'new' squadron retained the same role and aircraft. 'A' Flight was equipped with Anson C.12s and C.19s tasked with flying members of Government departments and Service ministries, and an air ambulance service. 'B' Flight was equipped with Proctor C.4 communications aircraft which were also used as hacks by RAF staff officers who wished to maintain their flying hours. At weekends they flew ATC cadets on air experience flights. 'B' Flight was also responsible for a number of exotic types assigned to the Squadron including a Hawker Tempest and no less than three Spitfires used by senior RAF officers. Spitfire PR.XIX PR659 was assigned to the AOC of Fighter Command, Air Chief Marshal Sir James Robb, who had taken part in the first RAF Tournament at Hendon. This particular

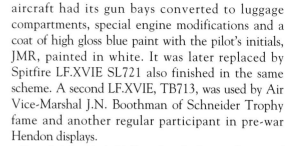

aircraft had its gun bays converted to luggage compartments, special engine modifications and a coat of high gloss blue paint with the pilot's initials, JMR, painted in white. It was later replaced by Spitfire LF.XVIE SL721 also finished in the same scheme. A second LF.XVIE, TB713, was used by Air Vice-Marshal J.N. Boothman of Schneider Trophy fame and another regular participant in pre-war Hendon displays.

For a brief period, 31 Squadron had one of a pair of captured German Brunswick Zaunkönig II STOL aircraft on its strength. Operated in RAF markings with the serial VX190, it was used as a station hack before being sold to a private flying club. The squadron was also responsible for the many visiting aircraft at Hendon which included French Air Force Ju-52s, Morane 472s and French and Dutch C-45s. Apart from the wartime-vintage types under 31 Squadron's charge, the squadron became one of the first RAF units to receive the new DH Devon C.1 in October 1948. One of the type's first sorties was an air ambulance flight taking an injured man from Barra in the Outer Hebrides, using the beach as a runway, to hospital on the mainland. The squadron was required to have an air ambulance, with a nursing orderly, on twenty-four-hour standby. Two of its Anson fleet were specially modified to carry stretchers with access doors in the roof.

The spring of 1949 saw the final departure of the Royal Auxiliary Air Force Squadrons from Hendon.

On 19 July 1948, the resident Metropolitan Communication Squadron was renumbered 31 Squadron. Here is the view from 31 Squadron's hangar, the old 'Royal Hangar', with some of its Proctor C.4s used for training.

A decision had been made that RAuxAF squadrons would trade-in their Spitfires for the latest generation of front-line jet fighters, Meteors and Vampires. In order to test Hendon's suitability for jet operations, John Cunningham borrowed a Vampire F.3 from the de Havilland factory at Hatfield, where he was employed as a test pilot, to make a series of 'touch and goes' on the airfield. In the event, he landed for a short time, but it came as no surprise, and a considerable relief to the local inhabitants, that he was unable to recommend the use of jets at Hendon. On 27 March 1949, 601 and 604 Squadrons took off from Hendon, from where they had operated for seventeen and fifteen years respectively, for the last time. The airfield again reverted to a transport and training role, although several other units would regularly appear and disappear during the next few years.

One of these units was the RAF Antarctic Flight which was formed on 25 April 1949. Hendon may seem an incongruous base for such a Flight and its two Auster Mk.6 seaplanes. However, the official reason for it being there was the station's proximity to London Docks and the Flight subsequently spent some months flight-testing the Austers, fitted with wheels, and their specialised equipment. The aircraft left for the Antarctic aboard a ship on 22 November to provide short range recce and landing support for the joint British/Norwegian/Swedish expedition to Queen Maud Land. Shortly after the arrival of the Antarctic Austers they were joined by others of the same type belonging to yet another RAuxAF unit. On 1 May, 661 Auxiliary Air Observation Post Squadron was reformed at RAF Kenley, one flight of which, No 1958, was destined to be the last flying unit to be formed at Hendon. Equipped with a mix of five Auster AOP.4/5/6s, the Flight was manned by ex-RAF pilots who had transferred to the Territorial Army, and continued the tradition of weekend flying at Hendon.

Hendon was one of many RAF stations that opened its doors to the public on 17 September to commemorate Battle of Britain Day. The event attracted more than 16,000 spectators.

By the end of the year, yet another long link with the airfield was severed when the United States Air Attaché's Flight departed to take up residence at Bovingdon. The US Embassy had first used the airfield in 1931.

In 1950 weekend flying increased with the arrival of No 142 Air Cadet Gliding School from RAF Hornchurch in February, and a new addition to 31 Squadron — a Tiger Moth. The biplane was used to supplement the Proctors giving Air Training Corps cadets air experience flights over the London area. On 26 October, 31 Squadron lost one of its Proctors when NP196 was written-off near Booker. The crew were uninjured.

The following year Hendon recaptured some of its former glories when it was chosen as the venue for

the Royal Aero Club's golden jubilee. The event, held in July 1951, was marked by a three-day exhibition and flying display sponsored by the *Daily Express* and entitled simply 'Fifty Years of Flying'. More than one hundred aircraft attended spanning the half century of flight, ranging from the Shuttleworth Collection's 1909 Blériot XI to the Bristol Sycamore helicopter then under evaluation for the RAF. Many of the veteran aircraft exhibited, especially those belonging to the Nash Collection and the Science Museum, were later to find a permanent home at Hendon. On Saturday 21 July, more than 50,000 people flocked to Hendon in perfect weather to enjoy the show. Among the crowds was Claude Grahame-White, making his first visit to Hendon for almost thirty years, and his old colleague Marcel Desoutter. They were rewarded

by the sight of a Blériot XI, Deperdussin and Blackburn Monoplanes, a Sopwith Pup and a Bristol Fighter taking part in the flying programme along with a Cierva C.30 autogiro, a Westland Dragonfly, the Sycamore, numerous gliders, a Supermarine Attacker FB.1, and aerobatic displays from teams of Royal Navy Sea Fury FB.11s from 802 Squadron, and Vampire FB.5s of 72 Squadron.

Vampires also provided the star attraction of the annual Battle of Britain 'At Home' display held on 15 September which, in contrast to the July event, was spoilt by bad weather and attendance suffered accordingly. The only other event of note during 1951 was the establishment in October of the Air Trooping and Freight Control Centre.

No 31 Squadron took delivery of two new types in 1952, the DH Chipmunk T.10, which replaced the

Tiger Moth and supplemented the Proctors for Cadet air experience flights, and for a short period, two Percival Prentice T.1s. The Secretary of State for Air, Lord de L'Isle and Dudley, learnt to fly on one of the squadron's Chipmunks using the name 'Mr Smith'. An aerobatic display by RAF Meteor F.8s drew more than 30,000 spectators to Hendon's Battle of Britain 'At Home' day on 20 September while the station was awarded the RAF Transport Command Accident Prevention Trophy for having an accident-free year.

The new year saw the East Coast of Britain and vast areas of Holland devastated by the worse floods in living memory. The large sum of money collected for the Lord Mayor of London's Flood Distress Fund was shared equally between the two countries and on 26 February, Queen Juliana and Prince Bernhard again flew into Hendon aboard the Dutch Royal Dakota, PH-PBA, to personally thank Queen Elizabeth for Britain's generous help during the disaster. In the same month, the US Navy unit VR-25 was redesignated Fleet Aircraft Service Squadron (FASRON) 76. The American presence at Hendon was also augmented by the arrival of support aircraft belonging to the US Army's 32nd Anti-aircraft Artillery Brigade in June. The unit was equipped with a selection of exotic types rarely seen in Britain including the L-17B Navion, L-19A Bird Dog, L-20A Beaver and the L-23A Twin Bonanza, used for staff transport and liaison flights around the United Kingdom and Europe. At the end of the year, RAF Hendon was again awarded the Transport Command Accident Prevention Trophy with 1.4 avoidable accidents per 10,000 hours flown. The one 'avoidable' accident was the loss of a 31 Squadron Anson C.19, VP538, which crashed at Turnhouse on 6 July.

Prince Bernhardt flew into Hendon on at least two more occasions during 1954 while the Duke of Edinburgh remained the most frequent Royal visitor, usually at the controls of the Queen's Flight Devon C.1, VP961, on which he received his multi-engine training. On more than one occasion Prince Philip was known to have travelled home from Hendon via the tube from Colindale to Green Park!

The annual Battle of Britain 'At Home' day in September attracted the largest crowd since 1945. Amongst the aircraft on static display was the Scottish Aviation Pioneer demonstrator wearing the serial XH496 while being evaluated by the RAF during Exercise 'Battle Royal'. The US Navy's FASRON 76 had yet another redesignation during the year when it became FASRON (Special) 200 equipped with Douglas R4D-6s and 8s, R5D-2s and Beech JRB-6s.

Hendon's resident RAF transport unit also underwent yet another name change when it reverted to its original title, the Metropolitan Communications Squadron on 1 March 1955. On the same date, 31 Squadron re-formed at Laarbruch in West Germany as a Canberra photo-reconnaissance unit. With the change of name came a change of emphasis. The Proctors were gradually phased out and by the end of the year the Squadron's strength was reduced to six Ansons, four Devons and four Chipmunks. Routine communications, air experience and continuation training continued to be the Squadron's main tasks, although its air ambulance capability was retained. Senior officers serving ground tours at the Air Ministry used the MCS to maintain their flying hours — five a year — to quality for flying pay. Some of them who had not flown regularly since the

end of the Second World War, or in some cases, the Western Front in 1917, came to Hendon to frighten the life out of the very junior officers who were detailed to sit in the right-hand seat to act as safety pilots. Air Marshals 'Bent Fred' Sowerby and 'Batchy' Atcherley, neither of whom were strangers to Hendon, were two of the most popular, experienced and terrifying of these hour-hunters.

Apart from the Duke of Edinburgh's now familiar Devon VP961, Prince Philip introduced another new type to Hendon when he arrived from Sandringham on 31 January 1955 aboard a DH Heron C.2, XG603. This aircraft, built at Hatfield

A frequent visitor to RAF Hendon in 1956 was the Queen's Flight's first Heron CC.3 XH375 with the Duke of Edinburgh aboard.

by the company that was established at Hendon, was destined to serve with the British Joint Services Mission in Washington, DC. However, Prince Philip was sufficiently impressed with it to order one for his personal use and on 24 May, only a few days after its delivery, the Prince flew Heron C.3 XH375 from Exeter to Hendon.

Another 'first' for Hendon was the appearance of 54 Squadron's new Hawker Hunter F.4s which thrilled a record crowd of over 50,000 at the Battle of Britain 'At Home' display on 17 September. On a more mundane level, but of no less local interest,

was the court martial of a number of airmen from Hendon's MT Section in December following the sale of an RAF crane to a scrap dealer in Watford. During the proceedings, it also came out that the MT Section had acquired the reputation of being the 'best spray shop for miles around', as long as you were prepared to have your vehicle finished in red, white or air force blue.

1956 was a relatively uneventful year for Hendon, although MCS Ansons made a number of dramatic air ambulance flights including one to the north west of England to collect a patient with a rare

A visiting US Navy UF-1A Albatross amphibian, 142361 assigned to the US Naval Attaché to Norway, seen at Hendon on 15 April 1956.

One of the more unusual aircraft attending the RAF Battle of Britain 'At Home' day at Hendon in September 1956 was the Commonwealth Trans-Antarctic Expedition DHC.3 Otter XL710.

disease for urgent treatment in London. The round-trip, from call-out to engine shut-down at Hendon, was completed in less than five hours. However, following another well-attended Battle of Britain display in September, at which the new Comet C.2, then entering RAF service, made a low pass and the RAF's sole DHC Otter, XL710, later used to support the British Commonwealth Trans-Antarctic Expedition, was on display in the static park, rumours that Hendon's days were numbered began to gain credence.

Confirmation of the station's rundown came soon after with the decision to transfer FASRON 200 to Blackbushe on 1 October, so ending fourteen years of uninterrupted US Navy operations at Hendon. By the end of the year, the Metropolitan Communications Squadron began to transfer some of its operations from the 'Sunken Garden', as Hendon was known to MCS crews, to nearby Northolt. It was not uncommon for an Anson to collect a few yards of railway telephone wire around the tail wheel during approaches and a long standing joke was that the runway overshoot was the foyer of Colindale's Odeon cinema. Despite the often appalling weather and lack of modern navaids at Hendon, the MCS in all its guises, had an exceptionally good safety record. Nevertheless, the number of movements

Two of the Metropolitan Communications Flight's aircraft, a Devon C.1 and Anson C.19 pose in Claude Grahame-White's original hangar on the last day of flying at RAF Hendon, 4 November 1957.

Three types operated by the Metropolitan Communications Flight, formed when 31 Squadron was disbanded in March 1955. Chipmunk T.10 WZ875, Anson C.19 TX875 and Devon C.1 VP952, on the apron in front of the original pre-WW1 control tower for the last time on 4 November 1957.

at the airfield were considerably reduced during the spring of 1957 when the 'weekenders', 1958 Flight, was disbanded on 10 March and a month later the US Army unit left for Bovingdon.

With the announcement that flying at Hendon would cease before the year was out, the largest crowd to visit the airfield since the last RAF Display

twenty years earlier attended the Battle of Britain 'At Home' display on 14 September. Although many people had hoped that a major air show would be mounted at Hendon to mark the end of its life as an active airfield, in the event only three aircraft from the Metropolitan Communication Squadron, an Anson, Devon and Chipmunk, took part in the closing flypast on 4 November.

7 GROUNDED

LONDON RECLAIMS THE AIRFIELD

Even before the last Metropolitan Communications Squadron Anson had been ferried from Hendon to Kemble for disposal, efforts to keep the airfield open for flying were being made. Proposals for its future ranged from the stationing of an RAF helicopter Wing at the base, while on 6 November, only two days after flying ceased, Hawker Siddeley discussed the possibility of using Hendon as a development base for its unique vertical take-off fighter, the P.1127, subsequently named Kestrel — the forerunner of the RAF's Harrier. The latter suggestion was, not surprisingly in view of the close proximity of suburbia to the airfield, not taken very seriously by the Air Ministry which had already decided to sell off most of the airfield.

However, there was at this stage no thought of closing Hendon as an RAF Station which was planned to remain open to house various non-flying units for the foreseeable future. To this end, the Joint Service Air Trooping Centre was established on 1 April 1958 to provide the co-ordination, flight planning and passenger handling of Long Range air trooping by chartered flights. The unit, which replaced the Air Trooping and Freight Control Centre at Hendon, comprised an RAF transit accommodation facility and a tri-Service manned Movement Control Wing based at the airfield. Passengers reporting for Long Range flights were moved by coach to the station, where the JSATC was responsible for feeding and flight processing them before onward movement to Blackbushe, Stansted or Gatwick for charter flights by Eagle or Caledonian Airways.

Almost exactly a year after the last MCS aircraft left, flying again resumed with the establishment of No 617 Gliding School for a trial period of six months to evaluate the suitability of RAF Hendon as an additional gliding site for HQ Air Cadets. Incidentally, 120 (Hendon) Squadron Air Training Corps had been resident on the airfield since 1949. No 617 GS was equipped with three T.21 Sedberghs and one T.31 Kirby Cadet and its first operational flight took place on 11 January 1959. However, due to the fact that the airfield was now directly under the GCA flight path of aircraft entering and leaving RAF Northolt, and both stations were in the London Heathrow TMA Air Traffic Control Zone, severe restrictions were placed on glider flying. These included: no soaring, no flying above 800ft, flying above 500ft limited to a maximum of two minutes, no gliding when aircraft on approach to Northolt, no gliding when Heathrow was operating from runway 23, approach angles not less than 1 in 10, and no gliding on weekdays.

During the six month trial period the last three restrictions were lifted and 617 GS, housed in one of the original ex-RAuxAF Belfast hangars, was able to carry out over 500 flights from the airfield. Soon after the cessation of powered flying at Hendon, the airfield had been sold to Barnet Council for building land and for the next few years the Gliding School operated under continual threat of imminent closure with the lease of the airfield being extended by the Council almost on a month-to-month basis. In March 1959 a TV crew arrived on the airfield to film segments of a programme entitled *The Derisible Man*. Hendon's proximity to Elstree's film and TV studios would make it a popular backdrop for the film companies in the years to come.

On 19 August 1959, one of Britain's greatest aviation pioneers and the founding father of Hendon aerodrome, Claude Grahame-White died in a Nice hospital three days before his 80th birthday.

BEA Westland Whirlwind G-ANFH piloted by Capt Cameron, lands at Hendon to pick up bags of Royal Mail to fly it to Windsor on 9 September 1961, the 50th anniversary of the first Air Mail flight.

While the major flying activity on the airfield was confined to gliders, the empty hangars would occasionally echo to the sound of rotary-wing arrivals. On 11 May 1961 an RAF Belvedere HC.1 of 72 Squadron paid a brief visit but an event of more significance occurred on 9 September, the fiftieth anniversary of the first Air Mail. To celebrate the occasion a BEA Westland S.55, G-ANFH, flown by the manager of the airline's Helicopter Experimental Unit, Captain 'Jock' Cameron, flew in to Hendon to collect 47,000 items of mail, including one addressed to Her Majesty the Queen. Amongst the onlookers present to watch the helicopter lift-off for its eleven minute flight to Windsor Great Park was Frederick Cannon, one of Grahame-White's mechanics at Hendon at the time of the first aerial post flights in 1911. After touching down near the original site at noon, Captain Cameron handed over a special greetings card from the Mayor of Hendon to the Mayor of Windsor and the mail was taken to Windsor Post Office to be stamped with a commemorative date stamp to mark the occasion.

In the meantime RAF Hendon continued as a functioning station where almost 1,000 airmen lived and worked. As such, the various traditions were maintained including seasonal balls held in Hendon's distinctive mock-Tudor Officers' Mess. In July 1963, Claude Grahame-White's widow attended the Summer Ball as Guest-of-Honour.

It was perhaps inevitable, given Hendon's location directly beneath Northolt's glide path, that an aircraft should mistake the former for the latter and attempt a landing on Hendon's white-crossed runways. The first to do so was a Spanish Air Force C-54, the pilot of which made a touch and go on 4 May 1964 after realising the mistake at the last minute.

1965 was the airfield's busiest year since 1957 in terms of aircraft movements. No 617 GS carried out a total of 4,699 flights while a number of helicopters took part in a Battle of Britain Display held on 11 September when the Red Arrows aerobatic team broke through the overcast to entertain the crowd. The following year a new unit, the RAF Supply Control Centre, was established at Hendon. Located on the south side of the airfield alongside the original Grahame-White buildings, the centre's computers controlled all of the RAF's stores, equipment and material, located throughout the world. On 2 June that year, another C-54, 49076, this time belonging to the United States Air Force, touched down at Hendon. Unfortunately the Skymaster's pilot, Major Gutt, en route from Châteauroux in France to Northolt, did not realise his error until it was too late and he burst two tyres before his aircraft came to a reluctant halt before the massed washing lines of North London suburbia. The official explanation for the landing was that the pilot had received a fire warning and took appropriate

Gnat T.1s of the RAF Aerobatic Team, the Red Arrows, perform over RAF Hendon's closed runway on 11 September during the 1965 Battle of Britain display.

action! It departed safely the following day after repairs and a certain amount of weight shedding.

On the 25 January 1967, a Luftwaffe Noratlas flying from RNAS Brawdy to Northolt made an unannounced arrival. This time the pilot, Sgt Moerig based at Celle, admitted his mistake and took off again 3½ hours later. By mid-year as many as four USAF C-47s were to be seen on the airfield, but closer examination revealed that they were wooden mock-ups starring in the wartime film epic *The Dirty Dozen*. Several episodes of the TV series *The Planemakers* were filmed on the airfield and a realistic mock-up of a 'vertical take-off fighter prototype' built by the BBC props department, seen

being towed around the airfield and residing in the Grahame-White hangar led to speculation that Hendon was indeed about to become a Kestrel base.

However, the inevitable could no longer be delayed and for the second time in a decade, flying at Britain's most famous airfield ceased. On 31 March 1968, a 617 GS Slingsby T21 Sedbergh WB986 piloted by Chief Instructor W.J.S. Hammond, who had made the first ATC flight at Hendon, with OC 617 Flt Lt Bullen as passenger, made the last flight from RAF Hendon. The next day the School was re-deployed to RAF Bovingdon in Hertfordshire as Barnet Council at last commenced work on the Grahame Park housing

The only Luftwaffe aircraft to land at Hendon was this Noratlas transport. The pilot, Sgt Moerig, mistook Hendon for Northolt during a flight from RAF Brawdy.

'Dakotas' return to Hendon!
Wooden mockups of wartime
USAAF C-47s fooled many a
'spotter' during the filming of *The
Dirty Dozen* at the airfield in 1967.

estate that was planned to cover 90 per cent of the airfield.

Before the runways were finally torn up, however, one more aircraft was scheduled to land at Hendon, and it was one of the largest ever to do so. For many years plans had existed for the establishment of an RAF Museum at Hendon, when funds permitted, and with this in mind several historic aircraft, including a number from the Nash Collection, had been stored on the airfield along with a few of more recent vintage such as a Vampire F.3. The plan was now turning to reality as two of the 1915 Belfast hangars on the eastern boundary were earmarked to form the nucleus of the museum. Among the aircraft offered to the embryo museum was a recently retired

47 Squadron Beverley C.1, XH124. The most economical method of delivering the four-engined military freighter to its new home from RAF Abingdon was by air and on 19 June, a sizeable crowd gathered to watch the lumbering shape of the Beverley on a short low approach over the original Grahame-White hangar before touching down on the white cross. With no Air Traffic Control at the airfield, permission to land was given by airmen firing green Very lights and the local fire brigade had to be called out for the occasion. Luckily they were not needed although by the time the Beverley had come to halt after using only half the length of the main runway, its brakes were red hot.

The last RAF fixed-wing aircraft to land at RAF Hendon before the runways were torn up, was Beverley C.1 XH124 which landed on 19 June 1968. Note the Grahame-White hangar in left background, the original control tower in the centre, and the 'King's Flight'/MT hangar on the right. The Beverley was displayed outside the RAF Museum which opened on 15 November 1974, but was broken up in 1990.

The highlight of the year for many, however, was RAF Founder's Day held on 5 July as part of the Royal Air Force's 50th Anniversary celebrations. It was fitting that Hendon should be chosen as the venue for such an occasion which was attended by 2,000 ex-RAF members who were serving on 1 April 1918, and their relatives. Many knew Hendon intimately, having either served at the station or been involved in the pre-war RAF Displays, and spent a nostalgic day wandering in to the large marquees dedicated to the various units that were established on 1 April 1918. A static display included many of the aircraft destined for the RAF Museum while the flying display featured a Hawker Hart, the Battle of Britain Memorial Flight's Spitfire, Hurricane and Lancaster, Sioux, Whirlwind and Wessex helicopters, a Shackleton and a formation of Vulcans and Lightnings. Among the VIPs present were Air Chief-Marshal Sir Arthur 'Bomber' Harris, Lord Balfour of Inchrye — and Mrs M. Thatcher MP.

The event had been held against a background of construction and demolition work as the airfield was slowly but surely turned into a housing estate and by 1 November the last runway had been ripped up. It was therefore all the more surprising to see a small aircraft appear from the overcast and touch down on one of Hendon's remaining perimeter tracks on 22 December. The recently qualified private pilot of the Piper Cherokee, G-AVWD, flying from Blackbushe was forced down over the airfield by low cloud. The following day, a second Cherokee G-AVUR landed at Hendon bringing an experienced pilot to fly the first aircraft back to Blackbushe. Both took off successfully the same day to become definitely the last fixed-wing aircraft to use Hendon.

While building on the airfield continued apace, both on the housing estate and the ten acre site allocated to the RAF Museum, the fact that the Royal Air Force Station continued to operate, was often overlooked.

A Gladiator, Hurricane and Spitfire in the static park at the Founders' Day Air Display held at RAF Hendon on 5 July 1968.

Both the resident units, the computerised Supply Control Centre and the JSATC facilities of the Movements Wing HQ and the Airbridge House transit accommodation, remained the centre of a busy station, In 1970, the JSATC's role changed when it took over the responsibility for Short Range trooping and in turn handed over its responsibility for Long Range flight planning to the newly-formed Services Booking Centre.

The airfield remained a focal point of interest for many ex-airmen, one of whom was the former Canadian Premier, Lester Pearson. He had been posted to Hendon in 1917 but his flying training was cut short when he was run down by a bus in the blackout during an air raid on the station. In June 1970 he returned to appear in a documentary film on his life.

Years of planning and preparation by Dr John Tanner and Dr John Reid, an ex-RAF Officer architect, came to fruition on 15 November 1972 when Her Majesty the Queen opened the Royal Air Force Museum, thus ensuring that at least part of the historic airfield would be preserved for future generations. One part that was not to be saved was Grahame-White's London Flying Club buildings which were demolished in 1974 to make way for expansion of the Hendon Police College.

The occasional Battle of Britain flying display was still performed in the skies over the Museum during the late 1970s and '80s while 32 Squadron Gazelle helicopters based at Northolt, were frequent visitors ferrying VIP visitors to the site's helipad. Another helipad on the site of the Grahame-White factory airfield across Aerodrome Road, now occupied by the Police College, was constructed in 1980 for use by the Metropolitan Police Air Support Unit's twin-engined Bell 222 helicopters.

Every year since its opening many thousands of visitors from all over the World have passed through the preserved Grahame-White factory gates to the RAF Museum which was expanded with the opening of the Battle of Britain Museum in 1978, and in April 1983 the Bomber Command Museum was opened by Her Majesty Queen Elizabeth the Queen Mother with Marshal of the Royal Air Force Sir Arthur 'Bomber' Harris. It also became the venue for several Battle of Britain air displays and RAF flypasts commemorating various events in its history. On the occasion of the Golden Jubilee of Fighter, Bomber, Coastal and Training Commands in July 1986, again opened by the Queen Mother in the presence of no less than six Marshals of the Royal Air Force, the Battle of Britain Memorial Flight led a formation of four Tornadoes and four Hawks over Hendon. Thus the airfield's long association with the Royal Family was maintained and it was therefore fitting that the Queen Mother should be invited to attend the formal closure ceremony of RAF Hendon in its Diamond Jubilee Year on 1 April 1987.

One reason put forward for its closure was that its position in the middle of London's suburbia with a public road running through its centre made the Station, and the 3,000 transit passengers that passed through Airbridge House every month, vulnerable to any sort of terrorist threat. Another was that its position also made it an extremely valuable piece of real estate for any developer. What had not yet been decided was the fate of the historic Grahame-White hangars, control tower and workshops, and the World War One Officers' Mess. Were they to be preserved or demolished?

One decision that had been made was that both the JSATC and RAFSCC were to redeploy to RAF Stanbridge in Bedfordshire close to Luton Airport from where the majority of Short Range air trooping flights depart. In the months leading up to its closure, Hendon's last Station Commander, Wing Commander

Hendon's original control tower and factory building, later the 'Pageant Club' as they were on the eve of the closure of RAF Hendon in 1987.

W.G. Simpson, determined that its passing would not go unnoticed.

By some historical oversight RAF Station Hendon never possessed its own badge and just six months before its closure, Her Majesty the Queen authorised a Badge for the Station. An Upside Down dinner, beginning with liqueurs and ending with *hors d'oeuvres*, was held in the Officers' Mess on 13 March recalling the one held in January 1914 at the Royal Automobile Club to honour the first British airmen to loop-the-loop, B.C. Hucks and Gustav Hamel at Hendon. The guests included Mr D.J. Carr whose father, Major R.H. Carr AFC DFM, was Grahame-White's Chief Mechanic and the first British aviator to loop-the-loop in a British-built machine.

On the morning of the closure ceremony the Station accepted and exercised the Freedom of the Borough of Barnet. This final parade was joined by many members

The last RAF aircraft to land at RAF Hendon was Puma HC.1 XW206 flown by a 33 Squadron crew on 1 April 1987, the day the Station officially closed. It took off to return to RAF Odiham after the Closure Ceremony.

of 600, 601 and 604 Squadron Associations who considered Hendon as their Squadron's spiritual home. The Order of Proceedings planned for the Closure Ceremony included the presentation of the Freedom Scroll and Poniard by the Station Commander to Marshal of the RAF Sir Michael Beetham, followed by a flypast of ten historic aircraft; Lancaster, Hurricane, Spitfire, Rapide, Mosquito, Firefly, Dakota, Beech 18, Anson and Devon, and four Hawks. After the Beating of Retreat Ceremony by the Queen's Colour Squadron and RAF Central Band, the RAF Ensign was lowered for the final time at 5.55 pm. On the day, the weather conspired to thwart more than a year's work by Wing Commander Simpson and his organising team. To the great disappointment of not only those taking part in the ceremony, but to the many who travelled long distances to witness the proceedings, low cloud and persistent rain led to the cancellation of the flypast and the parade took place in the MT Hangar. Despite the severely curtailed programme, it was perhaps entirely appropriate that the Queen Mother should be present at the ceremony held in the more intimate surroundings of the original 'Royal' hangar.

The only aircraft seen in the gloomy grey skies overhead the station that day was a Luftwaffe Dornier Do 28 on approach to RAF Northolt and RAF Puma XW206 of 33 Squadron which was to have taken news cameramen aloft to film the flypast. When it lifted off shortly after 3 pm to return to its base at RAF Odiham, it became the very last aircraft ever to fly from RAF Station Hendon.

EPILOGUE

Although RAF Hendon officially closed on 1 April 1987, the last RAF personnel remained on site for more than a year. East Camp closed its gates in February 1988, its Officers' Mess and the 'Kings' MT hangar locally listed for preservation, while the 1910 Grahame-White hangar, factory building and adjacent control tower were put on the Statutory List of Buildings of Historical or Architectural Interest, which at the time gave hope for their survival.

In this view of Hendon's East Camp, the listed Grahame-White hangar can be seen in the centre with the control tower and factory buildings behind it.

Hendon's West Camp closed in August 1988 with its three main units, the Joint Services Air Trooping Centre, RAF Supply Control Centre and MT Flight, which provided RAF transport for use in London and for JSATC's Luton Airport trooping flights link, all relocating to RAF Stanbridge, Beds. As none of West Camp's buildings were listed, the site was immediately put on the market for development and two years later disappeared under the expansion of the Grahame Park housing estate.

In the meantime, the MoD and the London Borough of Barnet vacillated over the future of the historic East Camp site. Despite rumours that the mock-Tudor Officers' Mess would be sold as an hotel, and the Grahame-White hangar relocated to the RAF Museum site, they, along with the other listed buildings, were left to the elements and their condition seriously deteriorated. It was also reported that the Metropolitan Police would cross Aerodrome Road and acquire part of East Camp for a new headquarters building, and that during 1993, 'special forces' used buildings on the site, still MoD property, for realistic training.

With the site severely damaged by the elements, vandalism, and the 'realistic' special forces' training, still no firm decision had been made by March 1994, although contractors had begun to demolish some of Grahame-White's derelict workshops, Auxiliary Air Force buildings and the 'Kings' MT

hangar that had been earmarked for the RAF Museum. It will be a sad and ignominious end to one of the most important birthplaces of British aviation if the historic buildings of Hendon airfield are not preserved for future generations. But if they were not, Claude Grahame-White would probably not have been surprised.

The mock-Tudor Officers' Mess built in 1917 seen after RAF Hendon's closure seventy years later. In the background is the Metropolitan Police School.

The original Grahame-White
Aviation Company gates were
incorporated into the main gates
of the RAF Museum at Hendon.

INDEX

—